بسم الله الرحمن الرحيم

Published by
GLOBAL PUBLISHING
Gursel Mh. Darulaceze Cd. No: 9
Funya Sk. Eksioglu Is Merkezi B Blok D: 5
Okmeydani-Istanbul/Turkey
Phone: (+90 212) 320 86 00

Edited by
Jay Willoughby

Printed and bound by
Kelebek Matbaacilik
Litros Yolu No: 4/1-A
Topkapi - Istanbul/Turkey
Phone: (+90 212) 612 43 59

All translations from the Qur'an are from
The Noble Qur'an: a New Rendering of Its Meaning in English
by Hajj Abdalhaqq and Aisha Bewley, published by Bookwork,
Norwich, UK. 1420 CE/1999 AH.

www.harunyahya.com

NAMES
OF ALLAH

He is Allah—there is no diety but Him. He is the Knower
of the Unseen and the Visible. He is the All-Merciful, the Most
merciful. He is Allah—there is no deity but Him. He is the King,
the Most Pure, the Perfect Peace, the Trustworthy, the Safeguarder,
the Almighty, the Compeller, the Supremely Great. Glory be to
Allah above all they associate with Him. He is Allah—the Creator,
the Maker, the Giver of Form. To Him belong the Most Beautiful
Names. Everything in the heavens and Earth glorifies
Him. He is the Almighty, the All-Wise.
(Surat al-Hashr, 59:22-24)

HARUN YAHYA
July 2004

TO THE READER

A special chapter is assigned to the collapse of the theory of evolution because this theory constitutes the basis of all anti-spiritual philosophies. Since Darwinism rejects the fact of creation—and therefore, Allah's Existence—over the last 140 years it has caused many people to abandon their faith or fall into doubt. It is therefore an imperative service, a very important duty to show everyone that this theory is a deception. Since some readers may find the chance to read only one of our book, we think it appropriate to devote a chapter to summarize this subject.

All the author's books explain faith-related issues in light of Qur'anic verses, and invite readers to learn Allah's words and to live by them. All the subjects concerning Allah's verses are explained so as to leave no doubt or room for questions in the reader's mind. The books' sincere, plain, and fluent style ensure that everyone of every age and from every social group can easily understand them. Thanks to their effective, lucid narrative, they can be read at a one sitting. Even those who rigorously reject spirituality are influenced by the facts these books document and cannot refute the truthfulness of their contents.

This and all the other books by the author can be read individually, or discussed in a group. Readers eager to profit from the books will find discussion very useful, letting them relate their reflections and experiences to one another.

In addition, it will be a great service to Islam to contribute to the publication and reading of these books, written solely for the pleasure of Allah. The author's books are all extremely convincing. For this reason, to communicate true religion to others, one of the most effective methods is encouraging them to read these books.

We hope the reader will look through the reviews of his other books at the back of this book. His rich source material on faith-related issues is very useful, and a pleasure to read.

In these books, unlike some other books, you will not find the author's personal views, explanations based on dubious sources, styles that are unobservant of the respect and reverence due to sacred subjects, nor hopeless, pessimistic arguments that create doubts in the mind and deviations in the heart.

NAMES OF ALLAH

HARUN YAHYA

CONTENTS

HOW MUCH DO YOU KNOW ABOUT ALLAH, OUR CREATOR?...8

AL-'ADL 11	AL-HADI 66
AL-'AFUW 14	AL-KHAFIDH 68
AL-AKHIR 15	AL-HAFEEDH 70
AHKAM AL-HAKIMEEN 16	AL-HAKIM 72
AL-'ALEEM 17	AL-HAKEEM 73
AL-'ALEE 19	AL-HAQQ 75
AL-'ASIM 20	AL-KHALIQ 77
AL-'ADHEEM 22	AL-HALEEM 79
AL-'AZEEZ 24	AL-HAMEED 81
AL-BA'ITH 26	AL-HASEEB 83
AL-BAQI 28	AL-HAYY 85
AL-BARI' 29	AL-QABIDH 87
AL-BASEER 31	AL-QABIL 89
AL- BASIT 33	AL- QADEE 91
AL-BATIN 35	AL- QADEEM 93
AL- BADEE' 36	AL-QADEER 95
AL-BARR 38	AL-KAFI 97
AL-JAMI' 40	AL-QAHHAR 99
AL-JABBAR 42	AL-QA'IM 101
AD-DA'I 44	AL-QAREEB 103
AD-DAFI` 45	AL-QASIM 104
AD-DARR 47	AL-QAWEE 105
AR-RAHMAN AR-RAHEEM ..49	AL-KABEER 107
AL-AWWAL 51	AL-KAREEM 108
AL-FALIQ 52	AL-QUDDUS 110
AL-FASIL 54	AL-LATEEF 112
AL-FATIR 56	AL-MAKIR 114
AL- FATTAH 58	MALIK YAWM AD-DEEN ...116
AL-GHAFFAR 60	MALIK AL-MULK 118
AL-GHANI 62	AL-MAJEED 120
AL-KHABEER 64	AL-MALJA 121

AL-MALIK 123	AN-NASIR 185
AL-MATEEN 125	AN-NUR 187
AL-MAWLA 127	RABB AL-`ALIMEEN 191
AL-MU' AKHKHIR /	AR-RAFI' 193
AL-MUQADDEEM 129	AR-RAHMAN AR-RAHEEM .195
AL-MU`ADHDHIB . . . . . . . .`131	AR-RAQEEB 198
AL-MUHEET 133	AR-RA'UF 200
AL-MUDHHEEK/AL-MUBKI 134	AR-RAZZAQ 202
AL-MUWAFFEE 136	AS-SAMAD 204
AL-MUHSEE 138	AS-SADIQ 206
AL-MUHSIN 139	AS-SA'IQ 208
AL-MUHEE 141	AS-SANI' 210
AL-MUQALLIB 143	AS-SALAM 212
AL-MUKMIL 145	AS-SAMEE' 214
AL-MUQTADIR 146	ASH-SHAFEE 216
AL-MUNTAQIM 148	ASH-SHAFI' 217
AL-MUSAWWIR 150	ASH-SHARIH 219
AL-MUBASHSHIR 152	ASH-SHAHEED 221
AL-MUBAYYIN 154	ASH-SHAKUR 223
AL-MUDABBIR 156	AT-TAWWAB 225
AL-MU'MIN 158	AL-WAHID 227
AL-MUJEEB 161	AL-WARITH 229
AL-MUHAYMIN 163	AL-WASI' 231
AL-MUTA'ALEE 165	AL-WADUD 233
AL-MUTAKABBIR 167	AL-WAHHAB 234
AL-MUSAWWIR 169	AL-WAKEEL 235
AL-MUSTI`AN 171	AL-WALEE 237
AL-MUTAHHIR 173	DHU AL-JALAL WA
AL-MUYASSIR 175	AL-IKRAM 239
AL-MUZAKKEE 177	AZ-ZAHIR 240
AL-MUZAYYIN 178	THE DECEPTION OF
AL-MUDHHILL 180	EVOLUTION 242
AL-MUGHNEE 183	

HOW MUCH DO YOU KNOW ABOUT ALLAH, OUR CREATOR?

Who created you? Who granted you your body, your eyes, or the color of your hair? Who determined the shape of your body or the color of your eyes? Who created all other people, the heavens, Earth, and every living being in between? Who determined the order of the planets, the Sun, and the stars in the depths of space?

Your answers to all these questions will be the same: "Allah." When asked to other people, they will also answer: "Allah." Indeed, Allah informs us in the Qur'an that people will confess this fact, as follows:

If you ask them: "Who created the heavens and Earth and made the Sun and Moon subservient?" They will say: "Allah." So how have they been deluded [away from the truth]? (Surat al-'Ankabut, 29:61)

So, how well do you know our Creator, Who planned you and the entire universe with a delicate equilibrium? Are you aware that He sees and hears you every moment and knows your every act? Where do you think Allah is? Did He create you and then leave you to your own devices? Does He tell you how to live? Can you see Him? Has anyone talked with Him? What other creatures did He create? What kind of a life does He promise after death?

No doubt, many similar questions may be raised and you may answer them in your own way. While doing so, you will rely on what you have learned from your family or relatives, the people surrounding you, or the books you have read. Well, have you ever wondered if their answers are correct?

Everyone may put forward different views about Allah.

Conditioned by his education, a philosopher may formulate a definition that relies on his favorite philosophers' views. A housewife who is truly ignorant of Allah believes in what she hears from her neighbors. A writer who writes about Allah may have received no theological training or even not know a single verse of the Qur'an, His final revelation to humanity. Yet anybody who reads his book considers its every line as if it were absolutely correct, internalizes it, and, with great confidence, tells it to other people. The majority of people never wonder if what they have heard is incorrect or mistaken.

We need to remember that humanity is fallible and, therefore, people may act ignorantly. For this reason, in our endeavor to know Allah, we turn to the Qur'an, the most reliable and unique source, the just Book in which Allah explains everything a person needs to know. When we refer to it for the answer to the above questions, we see that Allah is everywhere. He is nearer to you than your jugular vein, witnesses and sees everything you do, hears every word you utter, knows your innermost prayer, and is beside you at every moment. Furthermore, Allah talks to His servants with whom He wishes to speak. For instance, the Qur'an relates that He talked to Prophet Musa (as) and preferred him to all other human beings alive at that time. Allah also created angels and jinn, as well as the afterlife, where each individual will have an eternal existence in the Hereafter. Allah also explains how we should live in order to attain Paradise after death.

This book, written to introduce you Allah, seeks to replace the vague, flawed, and insignificant information that you may have acquired over the years with the genuine faith described in the Qur'an so that you may come to know Allah, the All-Mighty, better and draw nearer to Him. Allah introduces Himself to humanity through the Qur'an He sent down 1,400 years ago and informs us of His beautiful names. The various examples and explanations contained therein display Allah's infinite wisdom, intelligence, and artistry.

The verses provided under each of Allah's names are from Allah, Who mentions and then explains that particular name. Under each name, you will find concise explanations reflecting the viewpoints that will remind you of some details about the name in question. Although these explanations are inadequate, for many volumes could be written about just one of His names, we will limit ourselves to concise ponderings that will broaden the reader's viewpoint.

The Names of Allah only conveys what is written in the Qur'an, for we have no knowledge about His names other than what He teaches us. Those that are out of our knowledge are, as is the case with everything else, in our Lord's Sight:

They said: "Glory be to You! We have no knowledge except what You have taught us. You are the All-Knowing, the All-Wise." (Surat al-Baqara, 2:32)

AL-'ADL
The Just, The Equitable

O You who believe! Show integrity for the sake of Allah, bearing witness with justice. Do not let hatred for a people incite you into not being just. **Be just.** That is closer to piety. Have fear [and awareness] of Allah. Allah is aware of what you do. (Surat al-Ma'ida, 5:8)

Allah is the most just judge. As His order encompasses the universe, He will show His justice to His servants both in this world and beyond. All the acts of Allah, Who is All-Seeing, All-Knowing, and All-Aware, are for a divine purpose and are just.

Allah will judge all of each person's deeds according to His justice. Allah informs us that those who engage in violence will be punished and that even a single good word will be rewarded. He will manifest His infinite justice in the Hereafter.

The difficulties that unbelievers make for Prophets and believers, as well as their slanderous accusations and sins, will not remain unanswered. All of these difficulties, which raise believers' ranks in Paradise, lead unbelievers to the lowest level of the Fire. On the Day of Judgment, Allah will set up the Just Balance, and no soul will be wronged in any way. Allah will call them to account by ending the time that He has granted them. Given that Allah, the All-Knowing, keeps His promise, all people will see the consequences of their wrong actions in the Hereafter. Thus, unbelievers will be punished severely, while those who remained true to Allah will be rewarded most bountifully. In one verse, Allah states the following:

Those who pledge their allegiance to you [the Prophet] pledge allegiance to Allah. Allah's hand is over their hands. He who breaks his pledge only breaks it against himself. But as for him who fulfils the contract he has made with Allah, We will pay him an immense reward. (Surat al-Fath, 48:10)

There is an important point to consider here: While pondering over His justice, do not compare it with the human concept of justice, for a faithless person, while passing judgment, may well comply with his whims and desires, remain under the influence of his feelings, or forget what has been done. Most importantly, one never knows what is in the other party's mind. But Allah, Who never errs or forgets, has assigned angels for every person in order to observe and record each of their acts and thoughts. In brief, Allah holds each person's soul in His hand. The Qur'an also reveals that our Lord, Who gives the best judgment, is infinitely just:

On the Day We summon every people with their records, those who are given their Book in their right hand will read their Book and will not be wronged by even the smallest speck. (Surat al-Isra', 17:71)

In the Hereafter, Allah will pay back all of the wrongdoing and plots hatched against believers. In this life, He may grant the unbelievers many blessings (e.g., wealth and possessions), yet these will only lead them to more evil. In the Qur'an, Allah states that believers must not be attracted to such blessings, for when compared with what awaits them in the Hereafter, the benefits of this short life are insignificant, especially when the infinite punishment of Hell awaits unbelievers.

In the Hereafter, each person's real abode, every soul will find itself confronted with all of its good deeds. Allah will manifest His justice in Hell and Paradise for all eternity. Ultimately, Allah will separate those who believe in Him from those who do not.

Say: "Our Lord will bring us all together and then will judge between us with the truth. He is the Just Decider, the All-Knowing." (Surah Saba, 34:26)

Allah commands believers to be just as follows:

Allah does not forbid you from being good to those who have not fought you in the religion or driven you from your homes, or from being just toward them. Allah loves those who are just. (Surat al-Mumtahana, 60:8)

Allah commands you to return to their owners the things you hold on trust and, when you judge between people, to judge with justice. How excellent is what Allah exhorts you to do! Allah is All-Hearing, All-Seeing. (Surat an-Nisa', 4:58)

They are people who listen to lies and consume ill-gotten gains. If they come to you, you can either judge between them or turn away from them. If you turn away from them, they cannot harm you in any way. But if you do judge, judge between them justly. Allah loves the just. (Surat al-Ma'ida, 5:42)

AL-'AFUW
The Pardoner

Whether you reveal a good act or keep it hidden, or pardon an evil act, **Allah is Ever-Pardoning,** All-Powerful. (Surat an-Nisa', 4:149)

People are fallible beings who may at any time think erroneously, make a wrong decision, or display a flawed attitude. But Allah, Who created humanity and is fully aware of these mistakes, forgives them. If He were not so forgiving, no soul would ever attain Paradise. Indeed, Allah calls attention to this fact, as follows:

If Allah were to punish people for their wrong actions, not a single creature would be left upon Earth, but He defers them until a predetermined time. When their specified time arrives, they cannot delay it for a single hour or bring it forward. (Surat an-Nahl, 16:61)

Yet we need to remember that Allah only forgives His sincere servants who turn to Him in repentance. Thus, those desiring His forgiveness must be sincere and resolute in their repentance. Allah makes it clear that He will not forgive those who repent but then return to their former ways without feeling any true regret. In one verse, Allah states the following:

Allah only accepts the repentance of those who do evil in ignorance and then quickly repent after doing it. Allah turns toward such people. Allah is All-Knowing, All-Wise. (Surat an-Nisa', 4:17)

AL-AKHIR
The Last; The One Who Exists After Everything Else Perishes

He is the First and **the Last**, the Outward and the Inward. He has knowledge of all things. (Surat al-Hadid, 57:3)

Allah created the universe from nothing and, ultimately, will return it to its initial state and destroy it. Nothing is immortal, for all living beings come into existence for a predetermined period of time and then die—everything, that is, except Allah, Who is the First and the Last and therefore without beginning or end.

Allah, the Creator of life and time, is not affected by any of matter's characteristics. Given that He is infinite, He will exist for all eternity, existed in the infinite past, and is unaffected by time and space. This fact is stressed in the Qur'an, as follows:

Everyone on it will pass away; but the Face of your Lord will remain, Master of Majesty and Generosity. (Surat ar-Rahman, 55:26-27)

AHKAM AL-HAKIMEEN
The Most Just Judge

Is Allah not **the Most Just Judge**? (Surat at-Tin, 95:8)

Allah passes judgment on each matter and concludes them. All events evolve and develop upon His command and wish. Each of His judgments contains many hidden divine purposes. However, most people do not really understand His commands, for, given their limited intelligence, their ability to do so is also limited. Furthermore, Allah is infinitely wise, exalted above time and space, and the One Who created and bound humanity to these concepts. A person can never know what will happen the next day or even in an hour. When Allah gives a command, however, He has total knowledge of all of its consequences, regardless of time or place. Consequently, Allah creates everything in compliance with His plan and for a divine purpose.

But unbelievers can never understand Allah's purposes, for they base their worldview on certain causes and then think that everything evolves randomly and coincidentally. Therefore, they fail to understand that Allah controls everything. Believers, however, strive to grasp the divine purposes in Allah's judgments and comprehend that He gives the best judgments. In the Qur'an, Allah commands the following:

> **Follow what has been revealed to you, and be steadfast until Allah's judgment comes. He is the Best of Judges. (Surah Yunus, 10:109)**
>
> **Nuh called out to his Lord and said: "My Lord, my son is one of my family. Your promise is surely the truth, and You are the Most Just Judge." (Surah Hud, 11:45)**

AL-'ALEEM
The All-Knowing

Both East and West belong to Allah, so wherever you turn, the Face of Allah is there. Allah is All-Encompassing, **All-Knowing**. (Surat al-Baqara, 2:115)

After people begin to think, they start to learn and, over time, accumulate more and more knowledge. Some specialize in certain fields, such as physics, philosophy, or history. All of this knowledge relates to the verb "to know," as we understand it. However, this verb also has a dimension that is far beyond humanity's grasp: how Allah knows things.

Allah, being the Creator, holds the knowledge of the heavens, Earth, and every being in between, as well as of all the laws regulating the universe and anything that happens, regardless of time or place. Moreover, His knowledge is boundless, for He knows the names of all new-born babies at any moment, every leaf falling from every tree, what will happen to each star in each galaxy, whatever happens in space at any moment, what is hidden in every living thing's DNA, and an infinite number of other things.

We must always keep the following fact in mind: In addition to what has been mentioned above, Allah knows all of our thoughts and our most secret acts. We assume that we alone are aware of our feelings, thoughts, or distress. But this is a delusion, for Allah, Who holds complete control over every point of the universe, knows what is in each person's mind and everything else. Indeed, the Qur'an informs us about Allah's infinite knowledge:

You will not attain true goodness until you give of what

you love. Whatever you give away, Allah knows it. (Surah 'Al Imran, 3:92)

Do you not see that everyone in the heavens and Earth glorifies Allah, as do the birds with their outspread wings? Each one knows its prayer and glorification. Allah knows what they do. (Surat an-Nur, 24:41)

And the sun runs to its resting place. That is the decree of the Almighty, the All-Knowing. (Surah Ya Sin, 36:38)

See how they wrap themselves round, trying to conceal their feelings from Him! No, indeed! When they wrap their garments round themselves, He knows what they keep secret and what they make public. He knows what their hearts contain. (Surah Hud, 11:5)

But they will never ever long for it, because of what they have done. Allah knows the wrongdoers. (Surat al-Baqara, 2:95)

You did not kill them; it was Allah Who killed them. You did not throw when you threw; it was Allah Who threw: so He might test the believers with this excellent trial from Him. Allah is All-Hearing, All-Knowing. (Surat al-Anfal, 8:17)

AL-'ALEE
The Most High

It does not befit Allah to address any human being except by inspiration or from behind a veil, or He sends a messenger who then reveals by His permission whatever He wills. **He is indeed Most High**, All-Wise. (Surat ash-Shura, 42:51)

Allah introduces Himself to us: Allah, the Creator of all the worlds and the sole Sovereign of the universe, is the Most High and the Possessor of the heavens, Earth, and everything in between. There is no deity but Him. High is He, Exalted above all that they associate (with Him). He is the Sovereign, the All-Powerful, and the Lord of the Ways of Ascent. Allah is Self-Sufficient, above all need.

All of the beautiful names belong to Allah, for He is the Owner of infinite beauty and infinite sublimity. A person can know Him only to the extent that He introduces Himself, and can appreciate Him through the verses of the Qur'an. In one verse, Allah describes this name in the following terms:

Allah, there is no deity but Him, the Living, the Self-Sustaining. He is not subject to drowsiness or sleep. Everything in the heavens and Earth belongs to Him. Who can intercede with Him except by His permission? He knows what is before them and what is behind them, but they cannot grasp any of His knowledge, except for what He wills. His Footstool encompasses the heavens and Earth, and their preservation does not tire Him. He is the Most High, the Magnificent. (Surat al-Baqara, 2:255)

AL-'ASIM
The Protector

He [Prophet Nuh's son] said: "I will seek refuge on a mountain that shall protect me from the water." Nuh said: **"There is no protector today from Allah's punishment but He Who has mercy…"** (Surah Hud, 11:43)

People, all of whom are inherently feeble, can encounter all sorts of difficulties at any time, such as an earthquake, flood, hurricane, or volcanic eruption. In addition, people are vulnerable to mental distress. In the face of these unfavorable events, they must consider the following: Regardless of their effort or strength, they can never avoid a threat unless Allah wills this. Allah, the most Compassionate, is the only Protector, as the Qur'an relates in the following verses:

Say: "Who rescues you from the darkness of the land and sea? You call upon Him humbly and secretly: 'If you rescue us from this, we will truly be among the thankful.'" Say: "Allah rescues you from it, and from every plight. Then you associate others with Him.'" (Surat al-An'am, 6:63-64)

People remember Allah when they are left alone, when they realize that neither material wealth nor powerful people can help them, or when they fall sick. Yet after these situations pass, they forget what happened to them and become ungrateful toward Allah. Such people, who insist upon ungratefulness despite Allah's protection, will see the truth when they face infinite punishment in Hell. Their situation is related, as follows:

As for those who show disdain and grow arrogant, He will

punish them with a painful punishment. They will not find any protector or helper for themselves besides Allah. (Surat an-Nisa', 4:173)

AL-'ADHEEM
The All-Glorious

Everything in the heavens and everything in Earth belongs to Him. He is the Most High, **the All-Glorious**. (Surat ash-Shura, 42:4)

Allah's might and grandeur is surely beyond humanity's grasp. Yet, within the limits of their wisdom, people can still see and grasp His might. Indeed, the entire universe abounds with countless examples that indicate His greatness. A closer look at our own planet will make people feel His sublimity.

The heavens carrying clouds that weigh many tons, mountains rising thousands of meters in the air, oceans harboring millions of living beings, a lightening flash and the noise of thunder following it, and billions of living beings that have submitted to Allah—all of these and countless other details are clear signs of Allah's existence.

To have a better grasp of our Lord's grandeur, let's move beyond the limits of our world and think: We live in an unbounded space, the universe, which contains billions of galaxies with countless billions of stars. We live in one of these galaxies on a planet called Earth, which rotates about its axis at a velocity of about 1.670 kilometers an hour. Just thinking on these vast figures make us realize that our existence in the universe is as insignificant as the existence of a dust particle on Earth.

As this example also reveals, people given to sincere contemplation can grasp the majesty of their Lord, Who creates billions of galaxies and holds all of them in His hand. In one verse, Allah informs us about His beautiful names:

Allah, there is no deity but Him, the Living, the Self-Sustaining. He is not subject to drowsiness or sleep. Everything in the heavens and Earth belongs to Him. Who can intercede with Him except by His permission? He knows what is before them and what is behind them, but they cannot grasp any of His knowledge, except for what He wills. His Footstool encompasses the heavens and Earth, and their preservation does not tire Him. He is the Most High, the All-Glorious. (Surat al-Baqara, 2:255)

AL-'AZEEZ
The Almighty

Do not imagine that Allah will break His promise to His Messengers. **Allah is the Almighty**, the Lord of Retribution. (Surah Ibrahim, 14:47)

This name of Allah expresses that He will always triumph and that He can never be refuted, for only He has true power. Allah created the universe's order, all of its laws (both known and unknown), and all beings on Earth. In the face of Allah's infinite power, which clearly manifests itself in the universe, the feebleness of every created being and thing is obvious. All that is created can only exist, survive, and act if He commands so.

No doubt, this feeling of feebleness also holds true for humanity. No matter how well-off, strong, and powerful people may be, each person is weak and helpless in Allah's sight. No possessions, money, or status can protect them from Allah's punishment; only those who surrender to Him, live by His orders, and strive to earn His consent will be protected. In the Qur'an, Allah promises to grant superiority to His loyal servants.

Allah has written: "I will be victorious, I and My Messengers." Allah is Most Strong, Almighty. (Surah al-Mujadala, 58:21)

... and He has sent down the Furqan. Those who reject Allah's Signs will have a terrible punishment. Allah is Almighty, Lord of Retribution. (Surah 'Al Imran, 3:4)

Allah bears witness that there is no deity but Him, as do the angels and the people of knowledge, upholding justice.

There is no deity but Him, the Almighty, the All-Wise. (Surah Al 'Imran, 3:18)

Do not be grieved by what they say. All might belongs to Allah. He is the All-Hearing, the All-Knowing. (Surah Yunus, 10:65)

A pertinent hadith of Prophet Muhammad (saas) relates:

A bedouin once said to the Prophet (saas): "Teach me something to say." The Prophet (saas) replied: "Say: 'There is no god but Allah, the One with no partner. Allah is the Greatest by far; much praise be to Him. The Lord of the Worlds be praised; and there is no power and no strength save in Allah the Almighty, the All-Wise.'" (Sahih Muslim)

AL-BA'ITH
The Resurrector

How can you reject Allah, when you were dead and then He gave you life, then He will make you die and then **give you life again**, and then you will be returned to Him? (Surat al-Baqara, 2:28)

All people who have or will ever live are mortal. Everyone dies and is buried. Despite this obvious fact, however, most people avoid thinking about death and their subsequent resurrection. The Qur'an describes their situation, as follows:

They will ask: "Are we to be restored to how we were when we have become perished, worm-eaten bones?" (Surat an-Nazi'at, 79:10-11)

The Qur'an provides the most explicit answer to this popular delusion by proclaiming:

He makes likenesses of Us and forgets his own creation, asking: "Who will give life to bones when they are decayed?" Say: "He Who made them in the first place will bring them back to life. He has total knowledge of each created thing." (Surah Ya Sin, 36:78-79)

As these verses indicate, Allah created humanity and granted different qualities to everyone. Indeed, down to his or her fingerprints, each person has unique characteristics. As our Creator, He can re-create each person in the very same manner as many times as He wills. Allah displays this coming resurrection each autumn, when nature begins to "die" and then actually experience a type of "death" during winter. Yet when spring comes, we see dry branches blossoming, nature being revived and becoming green all over. Furthermore, this "resurrection" has been happening without any interruption since time began. For Allah, resurrecting each person is as easy as this. The parallel features of these two resurrections are stated in several verses, as follows:

> **He brings forth the living from the dead and the dead from the living, and brings Earth to life after it was dead. In the same way, you too will be brought forth. (Surat ar-Rum, 30:19)**

> **So look at the effect of Allah's mercy, how He brings the dead Earth back to life. Truly, He is the One Who brings the dead to life. He has power over all things. (Surat ar-Rum, 30:50)**

Another meaning of the beautiful name *Al-Ba'ith* is "sending out Prophets." Allah sent Messengers to warn their people and bring good news in order to call them to the right path. He revealed books to some of his Messengers so that they could bring people out of the darkness of ignorance and into the light of true knowledge. No doubt, this is a great blessing of Allah to His servants. In the Qur'an, Allah relates that:

> **Mankind was a single community. Then Allah sent out Prophets bringing good news and giving warning, and with them He sent down the Book with truth to decide between people regarding their differences. (Surat al-Baqara, 2:213)**

> **Allah showed great kindness to the believers when He sent a Messenger to them from among themselves to recite His Signs to them and to purify and teach them the Book and Wisdom, even though before that they were clearly misguided. (Surah Al 'Imran, 3:164)**

AL-BAQI
The Everlasting

Everyone on it will pass away; but **the Face of your Lord will remain**, Master of Majesty and Generosity. (Surat ar-Rahman, 55:26-27)

All of creation has an end. People are born, live for a certain period of time, and then die. This is also true of plants and animals. For instance, a tree may live for hundreds of years and then fulfill its destiny by dying at its appointed time. Similarly, non-living things also will meet their end, for time wears them all out. In addition, what remains of ancient nations is only their ruins. Allah calls our attention to this fact: **"How many wrongdoing cities We destroyed, and now all their roofs and walls are fallen in; how many abandoned wells and stuccoed palaces!"** (Surat al-Hajj, 22:45)

The universe also has an end. All of the meteors, stars, and suns hurtling through space will one day exhaust their energy and disappear. Or, for another reason, Allah will destroy this universe and keep His promise regarding the Day of Judgment. He can do this, for He is the Creator and sole Owner of infinity, as the Qur'an reveals:

> **Anything you have been given is only the enjoyment of this world's life and finery. What is with Allah is better and longer lasting. So, will you not use your intellect? (Surat al-Qasas, 28:60)**

AL-BARI'
The Maker

He is Allah—the Creator, **the Maker**, the Giver of Form. To Him belong the Most Beautiful Names. Everything in the heavens and Earth glorifies Him. He is the Almighty, the All-Wise. (Surat al-Hashr, 59:24)

The universe is based upon equilibrium and harmony. As scientific developments reveal more of its mysteries, we learn more about this equilibrium and harmony. It is apparent that each system in the universe has been designed by a superior intelligence that created everything in an amazing way. For billions of years, this great harmony and order has existed among an infinite number of living and non-living beings.

When we examine life on Earth, we come across amazing details. Whether we recognize it or not, we are surrounded with countless signs of creation. For instance, the ratio of different gases in the atmosphere are ideal for the survival of all living beings. Human beings and animals inhale oxygen and exhale carbon dioxide. Although this process continues without interruption, the amount of oxygen never decreases and the amount of carbon dioxide never increases. Moreover, this amazing equilibrium is never disturbed, because contrary to human beings and animals, plants inhale carbon dioxide and exhale oxygen. Thus, the oxygen consumed by people and animals is replaced by plants, a process that preserves this equilibrium.

This example is only one of the countless signs of creation on Earth. Both the micro- and macro-universes abound with similar examples. The universe, and thus life on Earth, exists only because our Lord creates things in conformity with one another. One verse reads:

> **And when Musa said to his people: "My people, You wronged yourselves by adopting the [golden] calf, so turn toward your Maker and kill yourselves. That is the best thing for you in your Maker's sight." And He turned toward you. He is the Ever-Returning, the Most Merciful. (Surat al-Baqara, 2:54)**

AL-BASEER
The All-Seeing

Have they not looked at the birds above them, with wings outspread and folded back? Nothing holds them up but the All-Merciful. **He is the All-Seeing.** (Surat al-Mulk, 67:19)

Our human faculty of sight is limited. With the naked eye, we can see for only a few kilometers. But to achieve this, we need clear weather and to be standing on a high place. Yet no matter how convenient the conditions may be, we can see only a hazy image.

In some situations, and especially when people are alone, they assume that nobody sees them. Assuming that they will not have to account for their deeds, they feel encouraged to do whatever they wish. Furthermore, they think they will never suffer any consequence for their wrongdoing. But this is a great delusion, for Allah sees even the smallest act. While our eyesight is limited, Allah sees the room in which a person remains, the rooms surrounding that room, the entire house, the city and country that harbor that house, the continent in which that country is located, the entire Earth, all planets, space, and all other dimensions beyond it. In the Qur'an, Allah informs us that He is aware of everything:

You do not engage in any matter, recite any of the Qur'an, or do any action without Our witnessing you while you are occupied with it. Not even the smallest speck eludes your Lord, either on Earth or in Heaven. Nor is there anything smaller than that, or larger, which is not in a Clear Book. (Surah Yunus, 10:61)

Perform prayer and pay alms. Any good you send ahead for

yourselves, you will find with Allah. Certainly Allah sees what you do. (Surat al-Baqara, 2:110)

They have different ranks with Allah. Allah sees what they do. (Surah Al 'Imran, 3:163)

Those who adulterate Our Signs are not concealed from Us. Who is better—someone who will be thrown into the Fire or someone who will arrive in safety on the Day of Rising? Do what you like. He sees whatever you do. (Surah Fussilat, 41:40)

AL- BASIT
The Expander

Is there anyone who will make Allah a generous loan so that He can multiply it for him many times over? Allah both restricts and **expands**. And you will be returned to Him. (Surat al-Baqara, 2:245)

Allah grants spiritual and material abundance to those who believe in Him and who obey Him wholeheartedly. He removes the difficulties they face. Upon encountering any hardship, trouble, or sickness, believers take refuge only in Allah. As a reward for this, Allah eases their tasks while making things difficult for unbelievers.

The Qur'an provides many examples about this issue. For instance, Prophet Musa (as) and the Children of Israel were forced to leave Egypt due to Pharaoh's violence. However, Pharaoh followed them. During this flight, the Children of Israel, who were caught between Pharaoh's army and the sea, thought that they were finished. Yet, Allah answered Prophet Musa's (as) call, divided the waters, and made a dry path so they could escape. Allah also destroyed Pharaoh and his army, and made the Children of Israel their inheritors.

This was also a manifestation of the following situation: **"Those who make pilgrimage in the Way of Allah will find many places of refuge on Earth and ample sustenance. If anyone leaves his home, making pilgrimage to Allah and His Messenger, and death catches up with him, Allah will reward him. Allah is Ever-Forgiving, Most Merciful."** (Surat an-Nisa', 4:100) No doubt, Allah's promise has always been true—and will remain so—for His faithful servants. One verse reads:

> **Your Lord expands the provision of anyone He wills and restricts it. He is aware of and sees His servants. (Surat al-Isra', 17:30)**

AL-BATIN
The Inward; The Hidden

He is the First and the Last, the Outward and **the Inward**. He has knowledge of all things. (Surat al-Hadid, 57:3)

Look around your room. Everything you see has been designed and made by someone: the door, the CD-player, a picture hanging on the wall, the window, and so on. Now look through the window at the trees, the Sun, the sky, flying birds, and other people. If it is nighttime, you can watch the stars and the Moon. Knowing that everything in your room has been made, is it not clear that everything around you also has been designed?

The truth of this assertion is apparent. If you cannot claim that a picture hanging on the wall was made by coincidence, then you also cannot claim that the Sun, stars, and the Moon are the result of coincidence. Everything you see on Earth and in the sky has a designer, producer, and creator. Our Lord, Who created everything with great artistry, introduces Himself to us through His creation.

When you look through the window you cannot see Him. However, Allah's existence, power, and artistry is clearly seen in His creation. This is the meaning that *al-Batin* conveys to us. His existence and control is clear in every corner of the universe, yet no one can see Him unless He wills otherwise:

Eyesight cannot perceive Him, but He perceives eyesight. He is the All-Penetrating, the All-Aware. (Surat al-An'am, 6:103)

AL- BADEE'
The Originator; the Innovative Creator

The Originator of the heavens and Earth. When He decides on something, He just says to it, "Be!" and it is. (Surat al-Baqara, 2:117)

No matter how competent and intelligent people may be, any innovation or new idea is limited to their background and what they see around themselves. We enjoy five senses and cannot imagine a sixth sense. Moreover, we can use these senses only to a certain extent. For instance, we are utterly ignorant of what we cannot perceive. Accordingly, we cannot think, discover, or exercise our wisdom about something that does not exist on Earth, or in the universe as far as we know it.

Indeed, scientists develop some of their projects by imitating animals in nature and their flawless systems. For example, the dolphin's snout served as a model for the bows of modern ships, while radar works on the principle used by bats, namely, emitting very high frequency sound waves (ultrasound) to compensate for their poor eyesight. Such examples are legion. (For further reference, please see, Harun Yahya, *For Men of Understanding*, 3rd ed., [London: Ta-Ha Publishers Ltd., April 2003])

Allah's knowledge is unbounded. Everything that exists, whether visible or not to the naked eye, is the product of Allah's innovative creation. At a time when there was nothing, no universe, galaxies, planets, living beings, or even a single cell, He decided to create a flawless system consisting of atoms, molecules, cells, living beings, planets, stars, and galaxies. Upon His command "Be," the universe and all of its contents came into being based upon no model other than what He willed to be. From the micro-world, of which the humanity became aware after thousands of years, to the celestial bodies discovered during the twentieth century, all of these systems were designed by Allah and function according to His laws. This is related in the Qur'an, as follows:

> **Say: "My Lord has commanded justice. Stand and face Him in every mosque and call upon Him, making your religion sincerely His. As He originated you, so will you return." (Surat al-A'raf, 7:29)**
>
> **He is the Originator of the heavens and Earth. How could He have a son when He has no wife? He created all things and has knowledge of all things. (Surat al-An'am, 6:101)**

AL-BARR
The Beneficent; The All-Good

Beforehand we certainly used to call on Him because **He is the All-Good**, the Most Merciful. (Surat at-Tur, 52:28)

Allah created all people and placed them in a setting that is perfectly suitable for human life and that was designed to serve them. In Surat an-Nahl, Allah informs us about some of these blessings:

He created man from a drop of sperm, and yet he is an open challenger! And He created livestock. There is warmth for you in them and various uses, and some of them you eat. And there is beauty in them for you in the evening when you bring them home, and in the morning when you drive them out to graze. They carry your loads to lands you would never reach, except with great difficulty. Your Lord is All-Gentle, Most Merciful. And horses, mules, and donkeys both to ride and for adornment. And He creates other things you do not know. The Way should lead to Allah, but there are those who deviate from it. If He had willed, He could have guided every one of you. He sends down water from the sky, from which you drink and from which come the shrubs among which you graze your herds. And by it He makes crops grow for you, as well as olives, dates, grapes, and fruit of every kind. There is certainly a Sign in that for people who reflect. He has made night and day subservient to you, and the Sun and Moon and stars, all of which are subject to His command. There are certainly Signs in that for people who use their intellect. And also the things of varying colors He has

created for you in Earth. There is certainly a Sign in that for people who pay heed. He made the sea subservient to you so that you can eat fresh meat from it and bring out from it ornaments to wear. And you see the ships cleaving through it so that you can seek His bounty, and so that hopefully you will show thanks. He cast firmly embedded mountains on the ground so it would not move under you, and rivers and pathways so that hopefully you would be guided, and landmarks. And they are guided by the stars. (Surat an-Nahl, 16:4-16)

No doubt, one can never bring into being, possess, or attain any of the blessings mentioned above by his own efforts. However, Allah has granted all of these beauties to humanity as blessings to indicate His vast generosity toward His servants. In return for such goodness, what does He expect? In the remaining part of the sura, Allah answers that He expects humanity to heed and serve Him, as follows:

Is He Who creates like him who does not create? So will you not pay heed? If you tried to number Allah's blessings, you could never count them. Allah is Ever-Forgiving, Most Merciful. (Surat an-Nahl, 16:17-18)

AL-JAMI'
The Gatherer

"Our Lord, You are **the Gatherer** of mankind to a Day of which there is no doubt. Allah will not break His promise." (Surah Al 'Imran, 3:9)

This attribute of Allah expresses His control over all systems in the universe. As the Creator of all that exists, He has the power to make all the living and non-living beings obey Him and so can gather them wherever He wishes. In the Qur'an, Allah promises that He will gather believers together in this world:

Each person faces a particular direction, so race each other to the good. Wherever you are, Allah will bring you all together. Truly, Allah has power over all things. (Surat al-Baqara, 2:148)

However, the actual gathering will take place on the Day of Judgment, when all believers will enter His presence. Allah, Who knows the unbelievers who reject Him and His messengers, as well as their actions, will collect everyone who has ever lived by causing the Trumpet to be blown. Allah will gather all unbelievers to account for their deeds, and then will order them to be cast headlong into Hell, where they will be repaid in full for what they did.

In Paradise, Allah will reward His followers also in crowds. On that Day, He will gather His servants and their leaders to His presence. With their light streaming out in front of them and to their right, they will attain Paradise due to His grace and mercy. Meanwhile, just as in this world, He will keep the unbelievers in Hell together and let them argue with one another. Their impious spouses and idols will remain together and be repaid in a narrow corner of Hell. The unbelievers will be consumed with the pain of being driven to Hell along with their irreligious spouses and friends, upon whom they had relied so much. In the verse below, Allah informs us that He will gather Satan's followers together and herd them into Hell.

It has been sent down to you in the Book that when you hear Allah's Signs being rejected and mocked at by people, you must not sit with them until they start talking of other things. If you do [remain seated], you are just the same as them. Allah will gather all the hypocrites and unbelievers into Hell. (Surat an-Nisa', 4:140)

AL-JABBAR
The Irresistible; The Compeller

He is Allah—there is no deity but Him. He is the King, the Most Pure, the Perfect Peace, the Trustworthy, the Safeguarder, the Almighty, **the Compeller**, the Supremely Great. Glory be to Allah above all they associate with Him. (Surat al-Hashr, 59:23)

Unbelievers show their arrogance and rejection of Allah by claiming that they exist apart from and are independent of Allah, and by attributing some of His characteristics to themselves. However, if they would stop and think seriously about this claim for just a second, they would easily comprehend that they did not will themselves into existence, cannot know when they will die, and had no say in the formation of their physical traits. They would realize that whatever they possess, including their own bodies, are temporary and will ultimately disappear. All of this makes it obvious that humanity is weak and can neither possess nor control anything. Further contemplation will surely provide more evidence of this truth.

In the face of all these facts, one can readily see that being arrogant toward our Lord, the Creator, is both foolish and dangerous. In fact, a person needs to comprehend that Allah is All-Mighty and that He created everything from nothing, grants every person's characteristics and meets their needs, can take them all when He wills, and that all living beings will die while He alone will exist for all eternity. Once all of this is understood, people need to submit to their Owner, for Allah has the power to make all who rebel and turn against Him bow to Him whenever He wills.

Allah relates the example of the Companions of the Garden as a lesson to believers. One of these men, who had been spoiled by his prosperity and achievements, later recognized his weakness, thanks to the name of *al-Jabbar*, and confessed his wrongdoing. What happened to this man, who swore to himself that he would harvest in the morning, is related in the Qur'an, as follows:

So a visitation from your Lord came upon it while they slept, and in the morning it was like burnt land stripped bare. (Surat al-Qalam, 68:19-20)

But when they saw it, they said: "We must have lost our way. No, the truth is we are destitute!" The best of them said: "Did I not say to you: 'Why do you not glorify Allah?'" They said: "Glory be to our Lord! Truly we have been wrongdoers." They turned to face each other in mutual accusation. They said: "Woe to us! We were indeed inordinate. Maybe our Lord will give us something better than it in exchange. We entreat our Lord." Such is the punishment. And the punishment of the Hereafter is much greater, if they only knew. (Surat al-Qalam, 68:26-33)

AD-DA'I
The Caller

O you who believe! Respond to Allah and to the Messenger when **He calls** you to what will bring you to life! Know that Allah intervenes between a man and his heart, and that you will be gathered to Him. (Surat al-Anfal, 8:24)

People assume that they can take the best care of themselves and thus make the best decisions, set principles for themselves, and believe that their lives will be good if they adhere to these principles. But this is a great delusion, for Allah created humanity and is nearer to each person than his or her own jugular vein. A person may not know many things about himself; however, Allah encompasses everything about him, for He holds complete control over his seen and unseen features, his most inner thoughts, and his subconscious. Furthermore, a person can never know what she will face the next moment or may well forget some of her past experiences. But Allah, Who never forgets or errs, knows all that has happened—and ever will happen—in every person's life. For these very reasons, only Allah knows what is best for each person.

Indeed, Allah draws attention to this fact:

... It may be that you hate something when it is good for you, and it may be that you love something when it is bad for you. Allah knows, and you do not know. (Surat al-Baqara, 2:216)

For this reason, a person needs to respond to Allah and comply with the "path that will bring him to life." Allah made this path clear through the Qur'an, which He revealed to our Prophet (saas). In every verse, Allah gives a detailed account of how a person must conduct himself or herself in order to attain salvation.

AD-DAFI'
The Remover of Tribulations

And with Allah's permission, they routed them. Dawud killed Goliath, and Allah gave him kingship and wisdom and taught him whatever He willed. **If it were not for Allah's driving some people back by means of others, Earth would have been corrupted.** But Allah shows favor to all the worlds. (Surat al-Baqara, 2:251)

Allah, Who protects believers against all material and spiritual dangers, also grants them irrefutable power against all unbelievers, hypocrites, and idolaters. While unbelievers plan and plot, Allah moves against them. Driving their harm away, He makes the plotters suffer the consequences of their own plots.

Meanwhile, Allah divides unbelievers, makes them fight each another, and thereby causes them to lose their strength. Furthermore, He keeps those who hate Muslims apart from them and afflicts them with many disasters. The Qur'an relates this divine protection for believers, as follows:

Those who were expelled from their homes without any right, merely for saying: "Our Lord is Allah." If Allah had not driven some people back by means of others, monasteries, churches, synagogues, and mosques, where Allah's name is mentioned much, would have been pulled down and destroyed. Allah will certainly help those who help Him… (Surat al-Hajj, 22:40)

This aside, only Allah can repel all varieties of difficulty, disease, misgiving, Satan's promptings to evil, and many other disasters from believers. No doubt, each one of these represents Allah's overt and hidden help to humanity. He is very compassionate toward His servants, to those who take refuge in Him and seek His help and forgiveness.

AD-DARR
The Afflictor

Am I to take as deities instead of Him those whose intercession, **if the All-Merciful desires affliction for me**, will not help me at all and cannot save me? (Surah Ya Sin, 36:23)

A sudden death, an unexpected disease, a crop-destroying hurricane, an earthquake leveling an entire city, fears for the future, a traffic accident, stress, loss of possessions, jealousy, ageing... Such events are sources of grief, fear, and despair for those who are unaware of the Hereafter's existence and consider this worldly life to be their real life. No one is immune to such events, any one of which may be encountered at any time and completely change one's life.

Since we know that Allah is infinitely compassionate, what is the divine purpose for such ordeals? Allah sends hardship and trouble so that a person can grow spiritually. A person who has difficulty breathing can hardly be arrogant or humiliate others. Meanwhile, one who recovers from being bed-ridden or a financial loss fully understands the value of the restored health and possessions. Through difficulty and ease, Allah makes each person better appreciate His generous blessings.

One point deserves special mention here. If the person being tested has faith and knows that the life in the Hereafter is one's real abode, he knows that every difficulty is from Allah and thus meets it with patience. Meanwhile, he seeks help only from Allah, for he knows that only Allah can remove this trouble. This way, Allah causes His servants to draw nearer to Him and raise their ranks in the Hereafter.

However, the truth is otherwise for those who have no faith in the Hereafter. Allah will display His name *ad-Darr* in Hell especially to these people. Yet compared to what they will go through in Hell, whatever causes grief here will remain insignificant, for all mundane pains are temporary.

In Hell, where unbelievers will roast in fire, every time their skins are burned off, Allah will give them new skins so that they can taste the punishment again and again. Their only food will be a bitter thorny bush, and their only drink will be boiling water that tears their intestines. They will face death, but will never die. Instead, they will suffer severe and eternal pain. Beaten with iron cudgels and covered with beds of fire, they will be cast into the narrowest and darkest corner of Hell, where they will only be able to groan.

Unbelievers will ask Hell's custodians to ask their Lord to let them out and lessen their punishment for just one day. While punishing them and denying them any escape, Allah will make them see the blessings and bounty being enjoyed by the believers in Paradise. In one verse, Allah commands:

> **If you ask them: "Who created the heavens and Earth?" they will say: "Allah." Say: "So what do you think? If Allah desires harm for me, can those you call upon besides Allah remove His harm? Or if He desires mercy for me, can they withhold His mercy?" Say: "Allah is enough for me. All those who truly trust put their trust in Him." (Surat az-Zumar, 39:38)**

AR-RAHMAN AR-RAHEEM
The Most Gracious, the Most Merciful

And Ayyub, when he called out to his Lord: "Great harm has afflicted me, and **You are the Most Merciful of the merciful.**" (Surat al-Anbiya', 21:83)

As is the case with all other beings, we also exist in a state of need. Our existence depends on many conditions: oxygen to breathe, water and nutrients for our bodies' physical functions, for example. The list is endless, for an infinite number of details are essential for maintaining each person's physical existence.

However, all people can survive without giving much thought to meeting their needs. Everything they need for their bodies and their survival has already been provided and put to use. The first example that comes to mind is breathing. Oxygen is essential for survival, but who provides the right ratio of oxygen in the atmosphere? Or, who places the system that takes in this oxygen and processes it so that it can be conveyed to each cell? None of these can be attributed to anyone, for no one has any part in forming the atmosphere or one's respiration system.

This vital need being the foremost, every detail is designed in its most perfect and feasible form. At this point, we encounter a superior wisdom that designs all details and the infinite compassion that the Owner of this wisdom—Allah, the Most Merciful—shows to us.

Allah's mercy is not limited to meeting people's physical needs. Allah created people, placed them in the most suitable place, and, in return, only asked them to serve Him. He also told people how to do this and sent down books and Prophets for this very purpose. This way, Allah made Himself known and called them to religion and moral excellence. These are obvious signs of our Lord's infinite mercy.

AL-AWWAL
The First

He is the First and the Last, the Outward and the Inward. He has knowledge of all things. (Surat al-Hadid, 57:3)

Does the universe have a beginning? This question has occupied the minds of people for centuries. People who understand that the universe must have an owner believe that it must have a beginning. However, other people do not want to accept the Creator's existence and thus claim that the universe has no beginning. They assert that the universe has existed forever and will exist for all eternity. However, modern science proves that such an assertion is a great delusion.

Although many theses have been put forward for the universe's existence, scientific circles have reached the following consensus: In 1929, Edwin Hubble revealed that the universe is in a state of constant expansion. Following this, scientists deduced that if we reverse the concept of time, we can think of the expanding universe as a closely pressing system, like a shrinking giant star, for instance. In this case, we conclude that a universe that shrinks according to the concept of time ultimately reaches a point of oneness. That is, the universe came into existence when a single point expanded by means of a big explosion.

Given this, we can conclude that our universe has a beginning. Since such a flawless system has a beginning, it must have a designer. This means that the One Who designed the universe is the First and the Last, for He existed before everything and will continue to exist after everything else has ceased to exist. The Owner of this eternal power is Allah, for His name "The First" indicates that He existed before all living beings, planets, galaxies, the universe, and even time itself.

AL-FALIQ
The Opener, The Splitter

Allah splits the seed and kernel. He brings forth the living from the dead, and produces the dead out of the living. That is Allah, so how are you deluded? **He splits the sky at dawn,** and appoints the night as a time of stillness and the Sun and Moon as a means of reckoning. That is what the Almighty, the All-Knowing has ordained. (Surat al-An'am, 6:95-96)

Our planet contains many kinds of plants, each of which has seeds unique to itself. If you keep dry seeds in a room, they may remain unchanged for years. Yet once they are buried in the ground or another suitable place, they start to sprout and, one day, grow into a rose bush or a giant plane tree.

While it is amazing to see such variety coming from a "dry seed," even more amazing is the formation of a living being. For a tree to exist, its seed has to collect the necessary materials from the soil and begin to grow. But a seed cannot determine the amount of minerals and water it needs, nor can it decide to grow into a green plant or a fruit tree.

If we claim that a seed can make such decisions, then we have to accept that the seed is "talented." But we cannot seriously assert that any seed has such faculties. As the verses above inform us, only Allah "splits the seed and kernel." By His will, countless trees and plants come into existence. Indeed, another verse relates that Allah creates everything:

He sends down water from the sky, from which We bring forth growth of every kind, and from that We bring forth

the green shoots, and from them We bring forth close-packed seeds, and from the spathes of the date palm date clusters hanging down, and gardens of grapes and olives and pomegranates, both similar and dissimilar. Look at their fruits as they bear fruit and ripen. There are Signs in that for people who believe. (Surat al-An'am, 6:99)

AL-FASIL
He Who Distinguishes (in the best way)

As for those who believe and those who are Jews, Sabaeans, Christians, Magians, and associaters, **Allah will distinguish between them** on the Day of Rising. Allah is witness of all things. (Surat al-Hajj, 22:17)

Some people seek mundane goals all their lives. Forgetting about the Hereafter, they strive for those goals they deem to be good. While doing this, however, they forget their real responsibility: to serve Allah. In order to please and thereby to earn the good pleasure of the deities they associate with Allah, they put forth a lot of effort and think that they benefit themselves and others.

Some people, on the other hand, devote their lives to Allah by using all of the means and blessings He grants them to earn His good pleasure. They seek to attain the straight path, please Allah, and display the moral excellence He demands from His servants.

The Qur'an states that the situation of these two people will not be the same, as follows:

The blind and seeing are not the same, nor are darkness and light, nor are cool shade and fierce heat. The living and dead are not the same. Allah makes anyone He wills hear, but you cannot make those in the grave hear. (Surah Fatir, 35:19-22)

On the Day of Judgment, Allah will distinguish between these people who adhere to differing paths and make them aware of their situation. On that Day, everyone will be fully repaid for what they did, and He will manifest His infinite justice:

On the Day of Rising, your Lord will decide between them regarding everything about which they differed. (Surat as-Sajda, 32:25)

AL-FATIR
The Creator; The Originator

"O My Lord, You have granted power to me on Earth and taught me the true meaning of events. O **Originator of the heavens and Earth,** You are my Friend in this world and the next. So take me as a Muslim at my death, and join me to the people who are righteous." (Surah Yusuf, 12:101)

Earth has a special design that supports life. Its location in space and its special structure, which meets the needs of all living beings, make it clear that this planet is the product of a superior wisdom. Our planet's living beings show that an astonishing design is inherent in all of them. Gifted with an appropriate bodily structure, every living being lives in a suitable setting.

This aside, as we focus more on the details of their formation, the fact of creation appears more clearly. Each cell, the basic unit of every living being, has a perfect system and such a flawless order that it is a clear refutation of the unbelievers' claim that life somehow created itself or is the result of a series of coincidence.

All that we see around us carries traces of an intelligent and purposeful design—a design that belongs to our Creator: Allah. Our Lord's artistry is visible in any detail. Allah relates His system's inherent perfection, as follows:

He Who created the seven heavens in layers. You will not find any flaw in the creation of the All-Merciful. Look again—do you see any gaps? Then look again and again. Your sight will return to you dazzled and exhausted! (Surat al-Mulk, 67:3-4)

Say: "Am I to take anyone other than Allah as my protector, the Bringer into Being of the heavens and Earth, He Who feeds and is not fed?" Say: "I am commanded to be the first of the Muslims" and "Do not be among the idolaters."
(Surat al-An'am, 6:14)

Their Messengers said: "Is there any doubt about Allah, the Bringer into Being of the heavens and Earth? He summons you to forgive you for your wrong actions and to defer you until a specified time." They said: "You are nothing but human beings like ourselves who want to debar us from what our fathers worshipped; so bring us a clear authority."
(Surah Ibrahim, 14:10)

AL- FATTAH
The Opener

If only the people of the cities had had faith and fear, We would have opened up to them blessings from heaven and Earth. But they denied the truth, so We seized them for what they earned. (Surat al-A'raf, 7:96)

As the Opener, Allah tests people with hardship. However, He does not impose an unbearable burden on anyone. When Allah sends difficulty to His sincere servants, He also opens a way out. Moreover, after each test He sends ease. Indeed, Allah cites the hardships that our Prophet (saas) encountered, as follows:

Did We not expand your breast and remove your load, which weighed down your back? Did We not raise your renown high? For truly with hardship comes ease; truly with hardship comes ease. (Surat al-Inshirah, 94:1-6)

Allah gives many examples of the help He offers to believers. For example, He supported Prophet Musa (as) during his troubles and eased his way. When he asked Allah to let his brother Harun (as) accompany him on his mission to Pharaoh, Allah granted his request.

This is only one example of Allah's continuous support and help for believers. He eventually removes their hardships, even those that seem impossible to overcome. Yet, He makes the unbelievers' hearts narrow and constricted and withholds His blessings from them. No power can restore these blessings, for only Allah can grant them.

This aside, Allah opens the gates of torment for unbelievers, as follows:

... nor will they humble themselves until We open to them a gate to a harsh punishment in which they will at once be crushed by despair. (Surat al-Mu'minun, 23:76-77)

AL-GHAFFAR
The Forgiving

"I [Nuh] said: 'Ask forgiveness of your Lord. **Truly He is Endlessly Forgiving.**'" (Surah Nuh, 71:10)

Allah's forgiveness is infinite. He gives all of His servants countless opportunities to repent and thereby purify themselves. People can save themselves from the punishment of Hell by repenting for what they did in ignorance. If they turn sincerely to the Qur'an and scrupulously adhere to Allah's commands, they will find our Lord ever forgiving and most merciful, as stated below:
Why should Allah punish you if you are thankful and have faith?... (Surat an-Nisa', 4:147)
In fact, even ungrateful people who are ignorant of religion may enjoy many blessings because of His forgiveness and compassion, for:
If Allah were to take mankind to task for what they have earned, He would not leave a single creature crawling on it; but He defers them until a specified time. Then, when their time comes, Allah sees His servants! (Surah Fatir, 35:45)
Allah grants enough time for anyone who is willing to receive admonition. He sends Messengers who warn and inform them about what is allowed and what is prohibited. Those who insist on denial, despite His revelations, will surely be repaid.
... I am Ever-Forgiving to anyone who repents, has faith, acts rightly, and then is guided. (Surah Ta Ha, 20:82)
But to those who do evil in ignorance and then, after that, repent and put things right, to them your Lord is Ever-

Forgiving, Most Merciful. (Surat an-Nahl, 16:119)

O you who believe! Have fear of Allah and faith in His Messenger. He will give you a double portion of His mercy, grant you a Light by which to walk, and forgive you. Allah is Ever-Forgiving, Most Merciful. (Surat al-Hadid, 57:28)

AL-GHANI
The Self-Sufficient, The Rich Beyond Need

O mankind! You are the poor ones in need of Allah, whereas **Allah is the Rich Beyond Need**, the Praiseworthy. (Surah Fatir, 35:15)

Throughout history, insolent and arrogant people have displayed one common characteristic: their power and wealth. These people grew arrogant toward Allah, due to the blessings He granted to them, and turned their faces away from Him. Forgetting that Allah is the real owner of everything, they attempted to claim ownership over what He granted them out of His great kindness. They grew rebellious, directed pressure and violence against believers, and met His Messengers with great hostility. Ultimately, Allah seized them with an unbearable torment. For example, He caused some of them to be swallowed up by an earthquake and showed others that He is Rich Beyond Need. In one verse, Allah relates the situation of such nations, as follows:

> **That is because their Messengers brought them the Clear Signs, but they said: "Are human beings going to guide us?" So they were unbelievers and turned away. But Allah is completely independent of them. Allah is Rich Beyond Need, Praiseworthy. (Surat at-Taghabun, 64:6)**

These arrogant and unbelieving people fail to remember or grasp that only Allah, the sole Owner, actually owns all that exists. Allah informs us of this fact, as follows:

> **Whatever is in the heavens and in the earth belongs to Allah. We have instructed those given the Book before you,**

and you yourselves, to have fear [and awareness] of Allah. But if you are unbelievers, what is in the heavens and in the earth belongs to Allah. Allah is Rich Beyond Need, Praiseworthy. (Surat an-Nisa', 4:131)

The Qur'an informs us that these people, because they were well-off, had grown arrogant and thus had turned away from worshipping Allah and adhering to His Messengers. Prophet Musa (as) responded to them in the following manner:

Musa said: "If you were to be ungrateful, you and everyone on Earth, Allah is Rich Beyond Need, Praiseworthy." (Surah Ibrahim, 14:8)

As Allah informs us in many other verses, He is the real Owner of power and wealth. He is Rich Beyond Need of any being, but everything and everyone is in need of Him, as the Qur'an reveals below:

Have they not traveled in the land and seen the final fate of those before them? They were far greater than them in strength. Allah cannot be withstood in any way, either in the heavens or on Earth. He is All-Knowing, All-Powerful. (Surah Fatir, 35:44)

AL-KHABEER
The All-Aware

O you who believe! Have fear [and awareness] of Allah, and let each self look to what it has sent forward for tomorrow. Have fear [and awareness] of Allah. **Allah is aware of what you do.** (Surat al-Hashr, 59:18)

Humanity, bounded by time and space, can be aware of only what is visible. Our inability to step outside of these boundaries is one of our greatest weaknesses.

Allah, Who created humanity as well as space and time, is not bound by these concepts. Allah, Who is exalted above anything, naturally is aware of all that takes place in the universe, regardless of time or location. He knows how many stars are in a galaxy located millions of light years away, each celestial body's orbit as well as the information hidden inside a seed lying underground.

Allah also knows everything about people's lives: their actions, where they were born and where they will die, and for what purpose they strove. He even knows such small details as when they cried or laughed, as well as their most secret thoughts, for He created them. The Qur'an states:

Those who are tight-fisted with the bounty Allah has given them should not suppose that that is better for them. No indeed, it is worse for them! What they were tight-fisted with will be hung around their necks on the Day of Rising. Allah is the inheritor of the heavens and Earth, and is aware of what you do. (Surah Al 'Imran, 3:180)
Eyesight cannot perceive Him, but He perceives eyesight.

He is the All-Penetrating, the All-Aware. (Surat al-An'am, 6:103)

Put your trust in the Living, Who does not die, and glorify Him with praise. He is well aware of the wrong actions of His servants. (Surat al-Furqan, 25:58)

Truly Allah has knowledge of the Hour, sends down abundant rain, and knows what is in the womb. And no self knows what it will earn tomorrow or in which land it will die. Allah is All-Knowing, All-Aware. (Surah Luqman, 31:34)

AL-HADI
The Guide

And so that those who have been given knowledge will know it is the truth from their Lord and have faith in it, and their hearts will be humbled to Him. **Allah guides those who believe to a straight path.** (Surat al-Hajj, 22:54)

There are two kinds of people: those who know and so can appreciate Allah's power, and those who do not. The latter lead an ordinary life and die. Throughout their lives, they are reluctant to wonder why they exist or who created them, whether they have any responsibilities toward Him, or the infinite power of our Lord, Who created the entire universe, including them, from nothing. Instead, they busy themselves with such mundane issues as their education, how to get promoted at work, or their children's future. Of course such matters deserve some attention, but it is a great mistake to make them the goal of one's life. Such minor issues hinder people from seeing the countless miracles surrounding them. Furthermore, even if they can see these miracles, they shy away from pondering over them.

Those who feel the urge to get acquainted with the signs of Allah's existence and absolute power, and then begin to appreciate them, lead a totally different life. Out of their strong conscience, they observe their surroundings with awe and acknowledge that He created whatever they see. Aware of their responsibilities toward our Lord, the All-Mighty, they do what is pleasing to Allah, live according to His rules, and, most important of all, realize that each person will be called to account in the Hereafter.

Allah guides the members of the first group. Although they have always remained a minority, their way has always been the right one. Allah relates the difference between these two groups, as follows:

Those who believe in what has been sent down to you, what was sent down before you, and are certain about the Hereafter. They are the people guided by their Lord. They are the ones who have success. As for those who are unbelievers, it makes no difference to them whether you warn them or do not warn them, [for] they will not believe. Allah has sealed up their hearts and hearing, and over their eyes is a blindfold. They will meet with a terrible punishment. (Surat al-Baqara, 2:4-7)

No doubt, being one of these people is a great blessing granted by Allah, for unless otherwise willed by Him, no one can guide anyone else to the truth and the righteous path:

You cannot guide those you would like to, but Allah guides those He wills. He has best knowledge of the guided. (Surat al-Qasas, 28:56)

AL-KHAFIDH
The Abaser

Abasing [one party], exalting [the other] (Surat al-Waqi'a, 56:3)

Everyone can see, think, and draw conclusions from what they think. For instance, our body's flawless functioning indicates an intricate design. Considering the wisdom inherent in this design's details will make one realize that someone must have planned, designed, and created all of these intricacies.

This process holds true for those who use their faculties. However, other people pay no heed whatsoever to the incidents they encounter. Unfortunately, this second group represents the majority. As we said earlier, they are born, grow up, lead an ordinary life, and then die. However, Allah praises those who think and learn, and humiliates those who do not. As the Qur'an states:

> **Those who remember Allah, standing, sitting, and lying on their sides, and reflect on the creation of the heavens and Earth: "Our Lord, You have not created this for nothing. Glory be to You! So safeguard us from the punishment of the Fire. Our Lord, those You cast into the Fire You have indeed disgraced. The wrongdoers will have no helpers."**
> **(Surah Al 'Imran, 3:191-192)**

Allah exalts those people who think and take heed. True servants of Allah, they are distinguished from all others. Those who do not think and do not use the faculties with which Allah has blessed them, on the other hand, lead a simple life like that of the animals, for they seek only to meet their physical needs. Allah debases such people, for they choose this animal-like life by refusing to exercise their conscience and think. The Qur'an describes them in the following terms:

> **The likeness of those who are unbelievers is that of someone who yells out to something that cannot hear—it is nothing but a cry and a call. Deaf, dumb, and blind. They do not use their intellect. (Surat al-Baqara, 2:171)**

AL-HAFEEDH
The Guardian; The Preserver

"If you turn your backs, I have transmitted to you what I was sent to you with; my Lord will replace you with another people, and you will not harm Him at all. **My Lord is the Preserver of everything.**" (Surah Hud, 11:57)

Today, all of our scientific data indicates that the universe was brought into existence from nonexistence. Those atoms that existed when the universe first came into existence, and those that make up every living and non-living being today, are the very same atoms. Science further verifies that the number of atoms in existence has never changed. Those atoms, which spread at a tremendous speed throughout the universe after it came into existence, today make up stars, Earth, the air, water on Earth's surface and even in your body. The fact that they accomplish this with such a superior order reveals the existence of the Power that controls each atom, for the existence of this order necessitates the existence of the Power that establishes it.

At this point, we come across one fact: Allah, Who created matter from non-existence and established a flawless order, surely knows about each stage of this process, for even a single second of such an intricate and complex system could not have formed randomly. This fact reveals His infinite power. Moreover, He continues to observe and protect this order. The verse, **"Your Lord is always watching"** (Surah al-Fajr, 89:14) reveals Allah's everlasting protection of the universe:

We know exactly how the earth eats them away. We possess

an all-preserving Book. (Surat al-Qaf, 50:4)

He had no authority over them, except to enable Us to know those who believe in the Hereafter from those who are in doubt about it. Your Lord is the Preserver of all things. (Surah Saba, 34:21)

As for those who take others besides Him as protectors, Allah takes care of them. You are not set over them as a guardian. (Surat ash-Shura, 42:6)

The Prophet (saas) said:

"Be mindful of Allah and He will protect you. Be mindful of Allah, and you will find Him in front of you." (Hadith at-Tirmidhi)

AL- HAKIM
The Judge

"**Am I to desire someone other than Allah as a judge,** when it is He Who has sent down the Book to you clarifying everything?" Those We have given the Book know it has been sent down from your Lord with truth, so on no account be among the doubters. (Surat al-An'am, 6:114)

Allah created all people and placed them on Earth, a place of trial set up to distinguish the good people from the evil ones. He sent Messengers with books that would enable the people to distinguish right from wrong. Throughout history, all Messengers warned their peoples and summoned them to the straight path. But over time, people distorted these books by replacing parts of the divine messages with personal judgments designed to protect their own interests. Despite this, Allah sent down an incorruptible Qur'an as a "guide" to them: **"We have sent down the Reminder and will preserve it"** (Surat al-Hijr, 15:9).

The Qur'an is the sole reference for arriving at the truth, for only It is unique and contains all of His commands. Those who embrace this Book and strive to fulfill its commands have found the true path. Those who judge according to Allah's commands and fulfill His demands will be rewarded in the Hereafter.

AL- HAKEEM
The All-Wise

He is Allah—the Creator, the Maker, the Giver of Form. To Him belong the Most Beautiful Names. Everything in the heavens and Earth glorifies Him. He is the Almighty, **the All-Wise**. (Surat al-Hashr, 59:24)

As we mentioned earlier, everything around us contains obvious signs of creation. Galaxies proceed toward a certain direction, Earth follows a particular orbit, living organisms contain intricate systems discovered only recently, and events occur in perfect order in the micro-universe, which is invisible to the naked eye... As science proceeds, the cumulative information reveals ever more clearly the delicacy inherent in the universe's design.

Modern science has unearthed the following fact: All events that have occurred since the universe's creation have developed according to a particular plan. The end result is Earth and all of its inhabitants. Given this, all of us have the responsibility to recognize that we are surrounded with the most suitable conditions and to grasp the divine wisdom behind the universe's formation.

Living amidst such blessings, we need to remember that everything is created for a certain purpose. After all, we are living on a planet designed to meet all of our needs perfectly. Just thinking about this fact is enough to realize that everything has been created with wisdom. As the Qur'an states:

... **"Glory be to You! We have no knowledge except what You have taught us. You are the All-Knowing, the All-Wise." (Surat al-Baqara, 2:32)**

The men and women of the believers are friends of one another. They command what is right and forbid what is wrong, establish prayer and pay alms, and obey Allah and His Messenger. They are the people upon whom Allah will have mercy. Allah is Almighty, All-Wise. (Surat at-Tawba, 9:71)

Your Lord will gather them. He is All-Wise, All-Knowing. (Surat al-Hijr, 15:25)

AL-HAQQ
The Truth, The Real

That is because Allah—**He is the Truth**, and what you call upon besides Him is falsehood. Allah is the All-High, the Most Great. (Surah Luqman, 31:30)

As is the case with all living and non-living beings, space and time are also created concepts. In a moment when space and time were non-existent, the universe was suddenly created from non-existence, and from within this universe emerged the concepts of space and time. Indeed, as we go back in time, we encounter a limit that we can never cross: the moment the universe was created. Modern science has determined this limit to be 10-43 seconds after the moment the universe was created. Before this, space and time could not be defined.

At this point, we encounter a dimension in which space and time did not exist. As these two concepts that limit humanity were "created" at a certain time, spacelessness and timelessness existed before this "creation." The One Who created these concepts is Allah, Who is utterly exalted above them and, consequently, Everlasting. This fact never changes, for only He has genuine existence. Outside His existence, everything is mortal and doomed to perish. As the Qur'an informs us, the only Truth is Him:

High exalted be Allah, the King, the Real! Do not rush ahead with the Qur'an before its revelation to you is complete, and say: "My Lord, increase me in knowledge." (Surah Ta Ha, 20:114)

That is because Allah is the Real, gives life to the dead, and

has power over all things. (Surat al-Hajj, 22:6)
In that situation the only protection is from Allah, the Real. He gives the best reward and the best outcome. (Surat al-Kahf, 18:44)

The Prophet (saas) used to glorify our Lord, saying:

"You are the Truth, Your saying is the Truth, Your promise is the Truth, and the meeting with You is the Truth, and Paradise is the Truth, and the (Hell) Fire is the Truth." (Sahih Bukhari)

AL-KHALIQ
The Creator

Allah created every animal from water. Some of them go on their bellies, some of them on two legs, and some on four. **Allah creates whatever He wills.** Allah has power over all things. (Surat an-Nur, 24:45)

Bees accomplish their tasks perfectly. Worker bees construct the hive, ventilate it, and maintain a constant temperature in it. They also bring in the nutrients they collect from flowers. The queen bee, on the other hand, remains in the hive and ensures the community's continuity. The gnat larva changes its skin four times before it fully completes its development. Toward the end of the pupa period, the pupa cocoon, which is covered with a special viscous liquid that protects the gnat's head from contact with water, is torn at the top and the adult gnat climbs onto the water with only its feet touching it.

Bees and gnats are only two types of living beings on this planet. Yet, as is the case with all other living beings, Allah determines when they will be born, live, and die. From the time they are born, they live as Allah considers proper for them and commands them to live. Never do they transgress the boundaries of their assigned duties. This holds true for lizards that survive in deserts where the temperature reaches 50° Celsius (122° Fahrenheit), as well as for penguins living in polar regions where the temperature can drop far below -50° Celsius (-58° Fahrenheit) or sponges whose habitat is thousands of meters below the ocean's surface. The earlier ones also lived in the same way and the latter ones will continue to do so, for Allah determines a way of life for each living being. Therefore, no living being can determine how it will live, for this determination lies only with Allah, to Whom they all submit.

Humanity is a tiny part of life, a being Allah created from a drop of water and granted a way of life. Thus, only He can determine when a person will be born or die, control the aging process, or will one to be immune or susceptible to any weakness or disease. The unprecedented nature of His power and His control over everything is related in the Qur'an, as follows:

> **He is the Originator of the heavens and Earth. How could He have a son when He has no wife? He created all things and has knowledge of all things. (Surat al-An'am, 6:101)**
>
> **Say: "Who is the Lord of the heavens and Earth?" Say: "Allah." Say: "So why have you taken protectors apart from Him who possess no power to help or harm themselves?" Say: "Are the blind and the seeing equal? Or are darkness and light the same? Or have they assigned partners to Allah, Who creates as He creates, so that all creating seems the same to them?" Say: "Allah is the Creator of everything. He is the One, the All-Conquering." (Surat ar-Ra'd, 13:16)**
>
> **They will ask their skins: "Why did you testify against us?" and they will reply: "Allah gave us speech, as He has given speech to everything. He created you in the first place, and you will be returned to Him." (Surah Fussilat, 41:21)**

AL-HALEEM
The All-Clement, The Lenient

Those of you who turned their backs on the day the two armies clashed—it was Satan who made them slip for what they had done. But Allah has pardoned them. Allah is Ever-Forgiving, **Lenient**. (Surah Al 'Imran, 3:155)

The Qur'an, which Allah revealed from His Sight to humanity, is the last Just Book. It still exists in its pure and uncorrupted state, for He has promised to preserve it, and He always keeps His promises. In this Book, Allah explains how to serve Him, what is allowed and what is prohibited, gives the good news that those who devote their lives to Him and strive to earn His good pleasure will enter Paradise and remain therein forever, and that those who turn their backs upon Him will enter Hell and be punished for all eternity.

Yet despite these facts, the majority of people disregard the Qur'an, and some of them never pick it up at all. Ignoring Allah's verses, they indulge in this world's pleasures and never worry about having to account for themselves after death or their next life. Ignoring the limits that He has set, they do not display the moral excellence Allah expects from them, share their possessions with others, or help them when they are in need. Furthermore, when they are called to have faith in Allah, they claim to know what they are doing. Very few of them have a genuine faith in Allah and meticulously comply with His commands.

Some reflection upon these facts can help us comprehend Allah's infinite compassion and mercy. Although unbelievers intentionally turn their faces away from the just religion and transgress the limits set by Allah, He does not punish them right away. Rather, He grants them various blessings and allows them to live in abundance. Moreover, He gives them time so that they may see the truth and return to the straight path. Islam is easy to practice, another expression of Allah's infinite mercy. In addition, He does not hold people responsible for their forgetfulness or their mistakes, and does not impose any responsibility upon the blind, the lame, and the sick. He relieves people's burdens by instructing them about patience and trust in Him. All of these examples are enough to grasp Allah's infinite mercy and compassion and the unbelievers' ungratefulness.

We need to keep another point in mind as well: Allah is infinitely just and, both in this world and the next, He will recompense people according to the best of what they did. This attribute is related in several verses, as follows:

> **Allah will not take you to task for inadvertent statements in your oaths, but He will take you to task for the intention your hearts have made. Allah is Ever-Forgiving, Lenient. (Surat al-Baqara, 2:225)**
>
> **The seven heavens and Earth and everyone in them glorify Him. There is nothing that does not glorify Him with praise, but you do not understand their glorification. He is Lenient, Ever-Forgiving. (Surat al-Isra', 17:44)**
>
> **Allah keeps a firm hold on the heavens and Earth, preventing them from vanishing. And if they vanished, no one could then keep hold of them. Certainly He is Lenient, Ever-Forgiving. (Surah Fatir, 35:41)**

AL-HAMEED
The Praiseworthy

He sends down abundant rain, after they have lost all hope, and unfolds His mercy. He is the Protector, **the Praiseworthy**. (Surat ash-Shura, 42:28)

All plants and animals live and glorify Allah wherever He has placed them. A fish in the ocean or a cactus in the desert lead their lives with great submission, according to what Allah has determined for them, and their maintenance of His order indicates this glorification. Everything in the heavens and Earth, oceans consisting of tons of water, mountains rising thousands of meters, clouds drifting in the sky, and thunderstorms also glorify Allah and indicate His infinite knowledge and power. Yet those who do not believe fail to grasp this glorification, as stated below:

The seven heavens and Earth and everyone in them glorify Him. There is nothing that does not glorify Him with praise, but you do not understand their glorification. He is Lenient, Ever-Forgiving. (Surat al-Isra', 17:44)

On the other hand, believers grasp our Lord's greatness, glorify Him, and thank Him for the blessings He grants, for they know that He expects them to be thankful servants. Allah commands thus:

What is in the heavens and in the earth belongs to Allah. We have instructed those given the Book before you, and you yourselves to have fear [and awareness] of Allah. But if you do not believe, what is in the heavens and in the earth belongs to Allah. Allah is Rich Beyond Need, Praiseworthy. (Surat an-Nisa', 4:131)

Musa said: "If you were to be ungrateful, you and everyone on Earth, Allah is Rich Beyond Need, Praiseworthy." (Surah Ibrahim, 14:8)

Those who have been given knowledge see that what has been sent down to you from your Lord is the truth and that it guides to the Path of the Almighty, the Praiseworthy. (Surah Saba, 34:6)

AL-HASEEB
The Reckoner

Those who conveyed Allah's Message and had fear [and awareness] of Him, fearing no one except Allah. **Allah suffices as a Reckoner.** (Surat al-Ahzab, 33:39)

Allah creates us and forms each one of us in our mother's womb with such great care that all of us are unique beings. While we are unconscious and still gestating, Allah protects and feeds us. Those nine months spent in the mother's womb is utterly a dark period, for no one knows all of the miraculous events that occur during that time. Only Allah knows these events, for He knows each person from the moment he or she was a single cell until the moment of his or her death.

Allah witnesses and remembers each person's deeds and thoughts, for He controls both the inner thoughts and the outer deeds. In brief, He controls everyone's spirit.

People forget their acts and words, and their experiences become dim memories. For example, something that happened a decade ago often seems meaningless. It is as if a major part of our past experiences have been deleted. But on the Day of Judgment, Allah will cause us to confront all of our good and evil deeds. Thus, we need to remember that He is with us all the time. Allah informs us about His name *the Reckoner* in the following verses:

Then they are turned to Allah, their Master, the Real. Jurisdiction belongs to Him alone and He is the Swiftest of Reckoners. (Surat al-An'am, 6:62)

Keep a close check on orphans until they reach a marriage-

able age. Then, if you perceive that they have sound judgment, hand over their property to them. Do not consume it extravagantly and precipitately before they come of age. Those who are wealthy should abstain from it altogether. Those who are poor should use it sensibly and correctly. When you hand over their property to them, ensure that there are witnesses on their behalf. Allah suffices as a Reckoner. (Surat an-Nisa', 4:6)

AL-HAYY
The Living

He is the Living—there is no deity but Him—so call upon Him, making your religion sincerely His. Praise be to Allah, the Lord of all the worlds. (Surah Ghafir, 40:65)

Being weak, what we can actually do is very limited. After we are born, we spend 5-10 years developing our intelligence through education and need constant care. Later on, we spend a great deal of time meeting our bodily needs (e.g., sleeping, and working to acquire food, clothing, and a place to live) and keeping ourselves clean and fresh.

Almost one-quarter of our life is spent in sleep. No matter how much we resist the need to sleep and use that time to engage in other activities, we cannot endure sleep deprivation for more than a few days. Indeed, such a lack of sleep affects our nervous systems by leaving us drowsy and unable to concentrate, and leads to poor memory and physical performance. If sleep deprivation continues, mood swings may develop.

All creatures have a fragile nature. Allah, the Creator of all beings, is *al-Hayy* (The Living). He controls everything at every moment, knows everything, and has power over all things. He is not subject to drowsiness or sleep, and is exalted above all forms of weakness. He gives various weaknesses to His servants, and commands them to recognize these weaknesses, serve Him, and ask Him for everything. Given these inherent weaknesses, we turn to our Lord, aware that we cannot live for another second unless He wills it. Several verses inform us about this attribute, as follows:

Allah, there is no deity but Him, the Living, the Self-Sustaining. (Surah Al 'Imran, 3:2)

Put your trust in the Living, Who does not die, and glorify Him with praise. He is well aware of the wrong actions of His servants. (Surat al-Furqan, 25:58)

Faces will be humbled to the Living, the All-Sustaining, and anyone weighed down with wrongdoing will have failed. (Surah Ta Ha, 20:111)

AL-QABIDH
The Seizer, The Restricter

Is there anyone who will make Allah a generous loan so that He can multiply it for him many times over? Allah both **restricts** and expands. And you will be returned to Him. (Surat al-Baqara, 2:245)

Allah, the sole Owner of everything, created all beings and furnished Earth with blessings that will meet their needs. All forms of wealth actually belong to Him, for He is its sole owner. In this world, Allah does not grant wealth to everyone. Yet, both the well-off and the poor need to remember that Allah grants and owns everything.

Allah tests those people to whom He grants wealth by how they use this blessing, and expects them to be thankful. Meanwhile, He restricts the wealth of others as a test of their gratefulness to Him. Consequently, whatever people lack or possess are not gains for them; rather, they are a test from Allah to see whether they want the life of this world or the next.

So fear [and be aware] of Allah, as much as you are able to. Listen, obey, and spend for your own benefit. It is the people who are safe-guarded from the avarice of their own selves who are successful. If you make a generous loan to Allah, He will multiply it for you and forgive you... (Surat at-Taghabun, 64:16-17)

Allah also grants many spiritual blessings in this worldly life. When He wills, He may test people through the imperfections related to these blessings by creating various tests. On the other hand, due to their insistence upon unbelief, Allah may repay unbelievers in this world by willing them to experience trouble and anxiety in their hearts. In such a situation, people have to realize that Allah saves them from all forms of trouble and hardship. Just as He restricts, He also expands (*al-Basit*). To the hearts of His sincere servants who only turn to Him for help, Allah gives serenity, peace, and a feeling of relief. He supports them with His help, love, and mercy, and also alleviates their tasks. In the Qur'an, Allah reminds us that all hearts find peace only in the remembrance of our Lord, as follows:

Those who have faith and whose hearts find peace in the remembrance of Allah. Only in the remembrance of Allah can the heart find peace. (Surat ar-Ra'd, 13:28)

AL-QABIL
The Acceptor of Repentance

He accepts repentance from His servants, pardons evil acts, and knows what they do. (Surat ash-Shura, 42:25)

All human beings are very vulnerable, for we cannot survive unless all conditions essential for life are provided for us. And yet some people tend to grow insolent, arrogant, and ungrateful toward Allah, as the following verses indicate:

We offered the Trust to the heavens, Earth, and the mountains, but they refused to take it on and shrank from it. But man took it on. He is indeed wrongdoing and ignorant. (Surat al-Ahzab, 33:72)

Truly man is ungrateful to his Lord. (Surat al-'Adiyat, 100:6)

Allah is fully aware of this inherent evil tendency. He knows that humanity is fallible, ignorant, and ungrateful, and yet He is always compassionate and merciful toward people. Out of His compassion, He showed humanity the way to salvation: repentance.

Allah gives all of us countless opportunities to purify ourselves through repentance. Regardless of what we have done or of our former ungratefulness, we can attain salvation if we are sincere, remain true to Allah, fear and are aware of Allah, and truly repent.

This attribute is a clear indication of Allah's compassion and mercy upon people. Allah, Who is not in need of anything, wouldn't have forgiven anyone if He willed. But out of His infinite compassion, He knew that people would need this compassion and mercy, and so gave the good news that He would accept the repentance of any sincere person. As the Qur'an states:

Do they not know that Allah accepts repentance from His servants and acknowledges their alms, and that Allah is the Ever-Returning, the Most Merciful? (Surat at-Tawba, 9:104)

AL- QADEE
The Ruler; He Who Completes His Task

The Originator of the heavens and Earth. When He decides on something, **He just says to it: "Be!" and it is**. (Surat al-Baqara, 2:117)

Allah is infinitely powerful. As the verses inform us, He wills something into existence by saying "Be." No doubt this is an obvious manifestation of Allah's greatness and absolute control over the universe.

From humanity's perspective, all life on Earth operates according to the law of cause and effect. For instance, objects depend upon Earth's gravity to remain stationary, while ships float only because water holds them up. But Allah is exalted above all of these causes and effects, for He creates all causes and the ensuing effects within the framework of certain laws and cause-and-effect relations to reveal whether we are His true servants. No doubt, Allah can easily create things without a cause. Indeed in the Qur'an, Allah relates some of His miracles, such as the birth of Prophet 'Isa (as) without a father:

She [Maryam] said: "My Lord! How can I have a son when no man has ever touched me?" He said: "It will be so." Allah creates whatever He wills. When He decides on something, He just says to it: "Be!" and it is. (Surah Al 'Imran, 3:47)

Allah informs us that everything is possible when He commands "Be." That Allah has infinite power, owns the entire universe, and rules humanity is related in several verses, as follows:

The likeness of 'Isa in Allah's sight is the same as Adam. He created him from earth and then said to him: "Be!" and he was. (Surah Al 'Imran, 3:59)

He created the heavens and Earth with truth. The day He says "Be!" it is. His speech is Truth. The Kingdom will be His on the Day the Trumpet is blown, the Knower of the Unseen and the Visible. He is the All-Wise, the All-Aware. (Surat al-An'am, 6:73)

His command when He desires a thing is just to say to it: "Be!" and it is. (Surah Ya Sin, 36:82)

He gives life and causes to die. When He decides on something, He just says to it: "Be!" and it is. (Surat al-Ghafir, 40:68)

AL- QADEEM
The Giver of Advance Warning

He will say: "Do not argue in My presence when **I gave you advance warning of the Threat.**" (Surah Qaf, 50:28)

Allah, Who is infinitely just, sent Messengers to tell humanity about Him. Through the just Books He gave to His Messengers, He granted all people discrimination, taught them how to worship Him correctly, and made them aware of the morality that will earn His good pleasure. He provided knowledge of the Unseen: Death may come at any time, the Hour is drawing nigh, no one will be wronged while accounting for his or her deeds on the Day of Judgment, and those who reject Him in this world will be punished in the next world.

By means of such warnings, including **"No indeed! Truly it is a reminder, and whoever wills pays heed to it"** (Surah 'Abasa, 80:11-12), Allah states that we can learn from the Qur'an and be guided. In addition, He gives a detailed account of what happens to those who are ungrateful, as well as what happened to earlier communities of unbelievers, so that His servants can take heed. Allah commands thus:

> Leave the deniers, who live a life of ease, to Me, and tolerate them a little longer. With Us are shackles, a Blazing Fire, food that chokes, and a painful punishment on the Day the ground and mountains shake, and the mountains become like shifting dunes. We have sent you a Messenger to bear witness against you, just as We sent Pharaoh a Messenger. But Pharaoh disobeyed the Messenger, so We seized him

with terrible severity. How will you safeguard yourselves, if you are unbelievers, against a Day that will turn children grey, by which Heaven will be split apart? His promise will be fulfilled. This truly is a reminder, so let anyone who wills take the Way toward his Lord. (Surat al-Muzzammil, 73:11-19)**

As the verse above informs us, "anyone who wills can take the Way to Our Lord." However, those who insist on turning away deserve a grievous end, for Allah gives the most just judgment.

AL-QADEER
The Powerful

Among His Signs is that you see Earth laid bare and then, when We send down water on it, it quivers and swells. He Who gives it life is He Who gives life to the dead. Certainly **He has power over all things.** (Surah Fussilat, 41:39)

As Allah informs us in many verses, every event is known to Him, for He wills it into existence just by saying: "Be." He knows when each leaf falls, when each woman or female animal becomes pregnant, and whatever happens at any location in the universe. If He wills, He can replace an unbelieving society with a new one. He grants or withdraws enormous possessions to whomever He wills, punishes an unbelieving society at a time and by a method of His choice, and makes the ground infertile or dry and devoid of life. Nothing that exists can prevent Him from doing what He wills, for His power is infinite, as revealed in the following verses:

Have they not traveled in the land and seen the final fate of those before them? They were far greater than them in strength. Allah cannot be withstood in any way, either in the heavens or on Earth. He is All-Knowing, All-Powerful. (Surah Fatir, 35:44)

No! I swear by the Lord of the Easts and Wests that We have the power to replace them with something better than them. We will not be outstripped. (Surat al- Ma'arij, 70:40-41)

Just as He punishes an unbelieving nation, He has the power to grant mercy to His sincere servants. In the Qur'an, we find many examples of His power. As a manifestation of His name, *al-Qadeer*, Allah has always helped His sincere servants and shown them a way out of their hard and difficult situation. He saved Prophet Ibrahim (as) from a pit of fire, rescued Prophet Yusuf (as) from the depths of a well, and released Prophet Yunus (as) from the darkness in the fish's stomach. Similarly, Allah granted a child to Prophet Zakariyya (as) when he was old and his wife was infertile, and thereby manifested His power over everything. Throughout history, Allah has supported all of His Messengers and believers and helped them with His mercy and power in return for their patience and trust in Him.

AL-KAFI
The Sufficient One

Is Allah not sufficient for His servant? Yet they try to scare you with others apart from Him. If Allah misguides someone, he has no guide. (Surat az-Zumar, 39:36)

Those who do not have a firm belief in Allah are afraid of many things, such as other people and natural disasters. Others are obsessed with losing their possessions or their loved ones. However, Allah addresses those who have firm belief in Him as follows:

The Lord of the heavens and Earth and everything in between them, if you are people with certainty. There is no deity but Him—He gives life and causes to die—your Lord and the Lord of your forefathers, the previous peoples. (Surat ad-Dukhan, 44:7-8)

As Allah informs us, He is the One God. Believers are well aware that nothing can harm or help them without Allah's permission. In the face of hardship, they turn to Allah out of their awareness that only He will help and answer their prayers. They do so because they know that He is the Almighty and that all other beings are powerless, unless He wills otherwise.

Thus, for believers only Allah can answer their calls for help and guidance. This means that they have no need to fear any other being or person. About this issue, the latter part of the verse above, **"Is Allah not sufficient for His servant?"** reads as follows:

… **and if Allah guides someone, he cannot be misguided. Is Allah not Almighty, Exactor of Revenge? ... If you ask them: "Who created the heavens and Earth?" they will say:**

"Allah." Say: "So what do you think? If Allah desires harm for me, can those you call upon besides Allah remove His harm? Or if He desires mercy for me, can they withhold His mercy?" Say: "Allah is enough for me. All those who truly trust put their trust in Him." (Surat az-Zumar, 39:37-38)

AL-QAHHAR
The Crusher; The Subduer; The Dominator; The All-Conquering

On the Day Earth is changed to other-than-Earth, and the heavens likewise, and they parade before Allah, the One, **the All-Conquering**. (Surah Ibrahim, 14:48)

Just as Allah relieves us of our sufferings and gives relief to our hearts, He has the power to punish us. The Qur'an gives examples of nations that He caused to perish at a time when they did not expect it—in the early morning—for they turned away from the just religion and rebelled against Allah. He sent them hurricanes that destroyed their houses and rained stones of hard baked clay upon them. To those whom He warned, He sent thunderstorms to raze their cities and sent earthquakes to turn the land upside down. Allah ruined them by sending a great blast. Allah's punishment is incomparable to any other punishment.

These are some of the punishment that Allah makes people taste in this world. But Hell's unprecedented torments deserve more consideration. Those who fail to appreciate Allah's power and who remain ungrateful, despite His infinite mercy, will be punished in the Hereafter.

When Allah casts the unbelievers into the midst of the Blazing Fire, they will encounter a form of misery previously unknown: Every time their skins are burned off, Allah will replace them and build walls of fire above them. The pain experienced in this world is utterly insignificant compared to the one in Hell. Indeed, the Qur'an informs us that the people of Hell will plead to Allah to kill them so that their pain will end. In Hell, Allah will punish unbelievers with His infinite power. This promise, which is certain to happen, is related in the following verses:

He is the Absolute Master over His servants. He is the All-Wise, the All-Aware. (Surat al-An'am, 6:18)

Say: "Who is the Lord of the heavens and Earth?" Say: "Allah." Say: "So why have you taken protectors apart from Him who possess no power to help or harm themselves?" Say: "Are the blind and seeing equal? Or are darkness and light the same? Or have they assigned partners to Allah who create as He creates, so that all creating seems the same to them?" Say: "Allah is the Creator of everything. He is the One, the All-Conquering." (Surat ar-Ra'd, 13:16)

The Day when they will issue forth and when not one thing about them will be hidden from Allah. "To whom does the kingdom belong today? To Allah, the One, the Conqueror!" (Surah Ghafir, 40:16)

Allah manifests His attribute of *al-Qahhar* upon those people who deny and refuse to believe in the Hereafter. However, Allah is infinitely compassionate and merciful toward His servants. After His servants' sincere repentance, Allah forgives their sins. He helps His sincere servants in both worlds and supports them with feelings of mercy, peace, and trust. In the Qur'an, Allah reveals His blessings upon believers and informs us that He does not punish His sincere servants, as follows:

Why should Allah punish you if you are thankful and believe? Allah is always responsive to gratitude, All-Knowing. (Surat an-Nisa', 4:147)

AL-QA'IM
The Self-Sustaining

Allah, there is no deity but Him, the Living, **the Self-Sustaining**. (Surah Al 'Imran, 3:2)

Some people believe that Allah created the universe's flawless system and then left it to its own devices. Though not often expressed, people harbor this mistaken belief in their subconscious. Those who do not want to acknowledge their responsibility to Allah and do not perform the deeds that He demands from them believe that this belief provides a way to escape their responsibilities.

However, there are such causes and laws adorned with delicate details underlying all of existence that, such complex systems cannot proceed without a superior power supervising them. People who can hear, see, and deduce from these experiences recognize this fact immediately. Indeed, Allah relates that He is the One Who holds the heavens, Earth, and everything in between, as follows:

Allah keeps a firm hold on the heavens and Earth, preventing them from vanishing. And if they vanished, no one could then keep hold of them. Certainly He is Lenient, Ever-Forgiving. (Surah Fatir, 35:41)

As this verse states, Allah created the universe and keeps a firm hold on it. Life exists only because He holds sway over it. This is also true for the stability of the universe's extraordinarily intricate balances and the existence of the subtleties inherent in those systems. The Qur'an relates these facts, as follows:

Allah, there is no deity but Him, the Living, the Self-Sustaining. He is not subject to drowsiness or sleep.

Everything in the heavens and Earth belongs to Him. Who can intercede with Him except by His permission? He knows what is before them and what is behind them, but they cannot grasp any of His knowledge save what He wills. His Footstool encompasses the heavens and Earth, and their preservation does not tire Him. He is the Most High, the Magnificent. (Surat al-Baqara, 2:255)

Faces will be humbled to the Living, the All-Sustaining. And anyone weighed down with wrongdoing will have failed. (Surah Ta Ha, 20:111)

AL-QAREEB
The Nigh; The One Who Is Near

If My servants ask you about Me, **I am near**. I answer the call of the caller when he calls upon Me. They should therefore respond to Me and believe in Me, so that hopefully they will be rightly guided. (Surat al-Baqara, 2:186)

Those who fail to appreciate Allah in the way He should be appreciated, as well as those who do not live according to the Qur'an, have vague and inadequate information about His existence. When asked, these people state that Allah created the heavens and Earth. Yet they assume that He is in the heavens and thus very far from them, although He forms and designs each person. The fact is, however, He introduces Himself to His servants through the verses sent from His Sight. He reveals just how close He is to His servants, as follows:

We created man and know what his own self whispers to him. We are nearer to him than his jugular vein. (Surat al-Qaf, 50:16)

When two people are talking, the third is Allah; when three people are talking, the fourth is Allah. If one whispers, Allah hears it; if one moves a little, Allah sees it. Allah, Who knows all of a person's thoughts, is with each person while he or she is sitting, walking, or speaking. While engaging in all of these, people cannot see Allah, but He sees them.

... So ask His forgiveness and then repent to Him. My Lord is Close and Quick to Respond. (Surah Hud, 11:61)

Say: "If I am misguided, it is only to my detriment. But if I am guided, it is by what my Lord reveals to me. He is All-Hearing, Close-at-hand." (Surah Saba, 34:50)

AL-QASIM
He Who Shares; Who Allocates Blessings, Justice, and Wisdom

Is it, then, they who allocate the mercy of your Lord? **We have allocated their livelihood among them** in the life of the world and have raised some of them above others in rank so that some of them are subservient to others. But the mercy of your Lord is better than anything they amass. (Surat az-Zukhruf, 43:32)

Trees that have lived in the Amazon for hundreds of years, a herd of penguins living on a remote glacier-surrounded island, a 30-year-old cactus in the desert, ants feeding on the mushrooms they grow on a garden of rainforest leaves, and an army of living beings that have existed for millions of years... All living beings need nourishment. Some desperately need water, whereas some others can survive without water for years. Some like hot weather, while others cannot survive in such a climate even for a minute. Furthermore, for all these living beings to remain together on this planet, many conditions have to exist at the same time. Allah, the Creator of all living beings, provides for each living being's needs separately and from the same soil.

Allah manifests His infinite compassion and mercy by meeting the needs of all that exists and allocating His mercy among all living beings. Allah created various blessings for our survival and provides for all of our needs. Indeed, Allah calls attention to this important fact:

He has given you everything you have asked Him for. If you tried to number Allah's blessings, you could never count them. Man is indeed wrongdoing, ungrateful. (Surah Ibrahim, 14:34)

AL-QAWEE
The All-Strong

Such was the case with Pharaoh's people and those before them. They rejected Allah's Signs, so Allah seized them for their wrong actions. **Allah is Strong**, Severe in Retribution. (Surat al-Anfal, 8:52)

Throughout history, Allah sent Messengers to many nations and revealed the straight path to them. The Messengers told their people that Allah is the only God and that they need to fear Him, in the sense of being in awe of Him, and observe His commands. However, as Allah informs us in **"That was because their Messengers brought them the Clear Signs but they remained unbelievers. So Allah seized them. He is Most Strong, Severe in Retribution"** (Surah Ghafir, 40:22), most of the nations called Allah's wrath upon themselves by denying and rejecting His Messengers.

In every age, unbelievers rebelled against the Messengers, made their lives difficult, and insisted upon doing so until Allah punished them. Holding power, wealth, and status in this world made them regard themselves as right and encouraged them to insist upon their arrogance. But they forgot one important fact: Allah is the Almighty.

Unbelievers who fail to understand this important fact have nothing in their hearts and minds but the quest of greatness. They disregard the fact that Allah can demolish all of one's possessions by sending a storm, raze all crops by heavy rains, wipe out all of one's relatives by a microbe, and destroy one's wealth in countless ways. To conclude, Allah punishes them in both this world and the Hereafter. In the Qur'an, Allah says this about the unbelievers:

Some people set up equals to Allah, loving them as they should love Allah. But those who believe have greater love for Allah. If only you could see those who do wrong at the time when they see the punishment, and that truly all strength belongs to Allah, and that Allah is severe in punishment. (Surat al-Baqara, 2:165)

They do not measure Allah with His true measure. Allah is All-Strong, Almighty. (Surat al-Hajj, 22:74)

Allah sent back those who were unbelievers in their rage without their achieving any good at all. Allah saved the believers from having to fight. Allah is Most Strong, Almighty. (Surat al-Ahzab, 33:25)

Allah is infinitely merciful toward His servants, who can appreciate His superior morality, sublimity, and grandeur in the best possible way. The Qur'an states that believers are given the good news of Allah's mercy, as follows:

Their call there is: "Glory be to You, O Allah!" Their greeting there is: "Peace!" The end of their call is: "Praise be to Allah, the Lord of all the worlds!" (Surah Yunus, 10:10)

AL-KABEER
The Great

The Knower of the Unseen and the Visible, **the Most Great**, the High-Exalted. (Surat ar-Ra'd, 13:9)

Allah has all creatures under His control. He knows when a buried seed will sprout, the orbit of a comet approaching Earth, the exact time when a living being will be born or die, the orbits of the electrons rotating around an atom's nucleus, and everything else. With His infinite power, Allah has control over all the thoughts of all people, both in their subconscious as well as their intentions while doing something.

Allah predetermines every detail of a person's life. Given that only He knows the Unseen, His infinite wisdom, knowledge, forgiveness, compassion, and punishment is far beyond human comprehension. No one can make even a minor alteration to His decisions. If Allah wishes to send something harmful or good, no one can deflect it.

Humanity is obliged to bow with reverence before such a great power and take refuge in our Lord, the All-Wise, and ask for mercy from Him, for we cannot attain salvation until Allah has mercy upon us and forgives us. That He is the All-High and Most Great is stated in the following verses:

That is because Allah is the Real, and what you call upon apart from Him is false. Allah is the All-High, the Most Great. (Surat al-Hajj, 22:62)

That is because Allah—He is the Truth, and what you call upon besides Him is falsehood. Allah is the All-High, the Most Great. (Surah Luqman, 31:30)

AL-KAREEM
The Generous

Whoever gives thanks only does so to his own gain. Whoever is ungrateful, my Lord is Rich Beyond Need, Generous. (Surat an-Naml, 27:40)

Allah created the universe and formed it according to His own attributes. Everything that exists belongs to Him. All beauties and subtleties are manifestations of His wisdom. Like all other beings, we come into being by His will. Each person, once a lump of flesh in his or her mother's womb, is born, grows up, and manifests Allah's artistry with his or her beautiful face. Indeed Allah relates humanity's superiority, as follows:

O man! What has deluded you in respect of your Noble Lord? He Who created you, formed you, proportioned you, and assembled you in whatever way He willed. (Surat al-Infitar, 82:6-8)

Yet, although people can think, many of them never wonder how they came into being and who is responsible for the countless blessings surrounding them. The Qur'an asks:

Has man ever known a point of time when he was not something remembered? We created man from a mingled drop to test him, and made him able to hear and see. We guided him on the Way, whether he is thankful or unthankful. (Surat al-Insan, 76:1-3)

On the other hand, those who use their intellect wonder who created them, who is responsible for the infinite blessings that they could never have attained on their own, and who has enabled them to think, use their intellect, and perceive all that is around them. These people reach the following conclusion: Our Lord, Who created them and granted all of the superior blessings that they could never attain on their own, is very generous. This Creator is Allah, the Lord of the heavens and Earth, and He reminds people to:

Recite: In the Name of your Lord Who created, created man from a clot of blood. Recite: And your Lord is the Most Generous, He Who taught by the pen, taught man what he did not know. No indeed! Truly man is unbridled, seeing himself as self-sufficient. Truly it is to your Lord that you will return. (Surat al-'Alaq , 96:1-8)

In other words, each person is responsible for turning toward Allah, the Gracious Creator, in order to thank Him. Allah grants countless blessings and, in return, asks only that people serve Him and abandon their arrogance. Allah's sincere servants, all of whom assume and display this morality, will be generously rewarded for their virtuous conduct.

AL-QUDDUS
The Holy; The All-Pure

Everything in the heavens and everything in the earth glorifies Allah, the King, **the All-Pure**, the Almighty, the All-Wise. (Surat al-Jumu'a, 62:1)

Allah is the sole Creator of all that exists, whether in the various micro- and macro-universes. Many people fail to see this all-pervasive order and stability when they gaze around themselves.

As Allah states in **"Allah keeps a firm hold on the heavens and Earth, preventing them from vanishing. And if they vanished, no one could then keep hold of them"** (Surah Fatir, 35:41), He regulates and protects all of the various universes' existing systems.

Given that we are inherently feeble, we sometimes err, forget, make mistakes, and become heedless. We also have many weaknesses. For example, we need to take care of our bodies, which involves endless routines to keep them clean and fresh. If we become too tired, are deprived of sleep for a few days, or do not drink for a prolonged time, we become weak. Yet, Allah, Who possesses everything and owns the most beautiful names, is surely beyond all weaknesses. Allah's infinite power, wisdom, glory, and unbounded knowledge are related in the Qur'an, as follows:

Allah, there is no deity but Him, the Living, the Self-Sustaining. He is not subject to drowsiness or sleep. Everything in the heavens and Earth belongs to Him. Who can intercede with Him except by His permission? He knows what is before them and what is behind them, but they cannot grasp any of His knowledge save what He

wills. His Footstool encompasses the heavens and Earth, and their preservation does not tire Him. He is the Most High, the Magnificent. (Surat al-Baqara, 2:255)

And the Prophet (saas) used to say in his prayer, as related in the following hadith:

"Praise and Holiness to You, Lord of the angels and souls." (Sahih Muslim)

AL-LATEEF
The Gentle, The Subtle

Allah is very gentle with His servants. He provides for anyone He wills. He is the Most Strong, the Almighty. (Surat ash-Shura, 42:19)

As mentioned earlier, there are two kinds of people: those who submit to Allah and those who rebel against Him. Among humanity, He made a very few of them truly submissive to Him. In many verses, Allah relates that the majority of people will not have faith and will not attain the straight path. These people deserve Hell, for they adhered to Satan's path, failed to remember Allah, and denied His existence despite their own certainty. People who submit themselves to Allah and live for His good pleasure, on the other hand, lead a beautiful life both in this life and beyond. No doubt, Allah's sending His Messengers and Books in order to guide humanity is one of His favors. In the Qur'an, Allah's kindness to believers is stated, as follows:

Allah showed great kindness to the believers when He sent a Messenger to them from among themselves to recite His Signs to them, purify them, and teach them the Book and Wisdom, even though before that they were clearly misguided. (Surah Al 'Imran, 3:164)

Allah, Who is Gentle, also shows His kindness to His faithful servants by helping them. In the Qur'an, He gives many examples of His help and support to His sincere servants. One of these concerns Prophet Musa's (as) people, who were saved from Pharaoh's violence and made inheritors of the land. This fact is related in the following verses:

> Pharaoh exalted himself arrogantly in the land and divided its people into camps, oppressing one group of them by slaughtering their sons and letting their women live. He was one of the corrupters. We desired to show kindness to those who were oppressed in the land, to make them leaders, and to make them inheritors. (Surat al-Qasas, 28:4-5)

As the sole protector and helper of believers, Allah will help them in the Hereafter, transform their evil into good, and show them great kindness:

> They will say: "Beforehand we used to live in fear among our families. But Allah was gracious to us and safeguarded us from the punishment of the searing wind. Beforehand we certainly used to call on Him because He is the All-Good, the Most Merciful." (Surat at-Tur, 52:26-28)

> Does He Who created not then know? He is the Subtle, the All-Aware. (Surat al-Mulk, 67:14)

> Eyesight cannot perceive Him but He perceives eyesight. He is the Subtle, the All-Aware. (Surat al-An'am, 6:103)

> Do you not see that Allah sends down water from the sky and then, in the morning, the land is covered in green? Allah is All-Subtle, All-Aware. (Surat al-Hajj, 22:63)

> "My son, even if something weighs as little as a mustard-seed and is inside a rock, or anywhere else in the heavens or Earth, Allah will bring it out. Allah is the Subtle, All-Aware." (Surat al-Luqman, 31:16)

AL-MAKIR
The Planner

When those unbelievers were plotting against you to imprison you or to kill or expel you: they were plotting and Allah was plotting, but **Allah is the Best of Planners.** (Surat al-Anfal, 8:30)

Those who plotted against the just religion throughout history strove to distance people from it for their own selfish desires (e.g., greed for power, personal interests, and so on). In the Hereafter, they will be told: **"No, it was your scheming night and day when you commanded us to reject Allah and assign equals to Him."** (Surah Saba', 34:33) Yet there is a very important point that we need to remember here:

Those before them plotted, but all planning belongs to Allah. He knows what each self earns, and the unbelievers soon will know who has the Ultimate Abode. (Surat ar-Ra'd, 13:42)

As is related in the verse above, "all planning belongs to Allah." Thus, against all of the unbelievers' plots, Allah devises the best plan. Allah calls attention to the deadlock facing unbelievers:

They concocted their plots, but their plots were with Allah, even if they were such as to make the mountains vanish. (Surah Ibrahim, 14:46)

As this verse relates, Allah protects all believers from these pl ots. This is very easy for Allah, Who turns all plots against His Messengers and believers into failures and makes unbelievers suffer the ensuing dire consequences, for "... **Allah is swifter at plan-**

ning..." (Surah Yunus, 10:21)

No doubt, Allah creates every incident with a purpose and for the ultimate good. He uses the unbelievers' plots against believers to test them. He then extends His help to those servants who can discern the good and beauties in the events He creates, and turns all of these to their benefit.

MALIK YAWM AD-DEEN
The King of the Day of Judgment

The King of the Day of Judgment... (Surat al-Fatiha, 1:3)

On the Day of Judgment, people will be resurrected and gathered together to account for their deeds. On that Day, they will have neither the will nor the opportunity to pay attention to the people around them, whether they are their parents, spouses, or children. Due to this Day's fearsome nature, everyone will pay attention only to themselves, for:

What will convey to you what the Day of Judgment is? Again! What will convey to you what the Day of Judgment is? It is the Day when a self will have no power to help any other self in any way. The command that Day will be Allah's alone. (Surat al-Infitar, 82:17-19)

On that Day, anything to which a person attaches too much attention will be reduced to insignificance. From then on, any mundane relation or kinship will lose all importance, for the only value that will remain is one's faith in Allah. No one will be able to help another person, for only Allah, if He wills, can save a person from this detrimental situation.

Each of us will be alone before Allah's presence, the Owner of the Day of Judgment, just as we were alone when we were first created. Each of our deeds and thoughts will be displayed on the Day of Judgment, for He never forgets any detail, no matter how small. Allah creates a setting that befits His Honor and calls His servants to account. However, He saves anyone He wills through His mercy.

On this Day, when unbelievers will be overwhelmed by a

grievous regret, believers will be joyful and exuberant:

> ... On the Day when Allah will not disgrace the Prophet and those who had faith along with him... **(Surat at-Tahrim, 66:8)**

That is because **"Allah will certainly help Messengers and those who believe both in the life of the world and on the Day the witnesses appear."** (Surah Ghafir, 40:51)

The sole king of that Day is Allah, for He is the only One Who can command. The related verses read:

> There will be but one Great Blast, and then their eyes will open. They will say: "Alas for us! This is the Day of Reckoning!" This is the Day of Decision you used to deny. (Surat as-Saffat, 37:19-21)

> Woe that Day to the deniers, those who deny the Day of Reckoning. No one denies it except for every evil aggressor. (Surat al-Mutaffifin, 83:10-12)

MALIK AL-MULK
The Master of the Kingdom

Say: "O Allah! Master of the Kingdom! You give sovereignty to whoever You will and take sovereignty from whoever You will. You exalt whoever You will and abase whoever You will. All good is in Your hands. You have power over all things." (Surah Al 'Imran, 3:26)

When you look around, everything that you see has an owner. The chair on which you sit is made up atoms, each one of which was created by Allah. A flower grows by combining such favorable circumstances as sunlight, water, and so on, all of which are granted by Allah. The sea lying beyond your window and all its inhabitants exist only because Allah wills them to exist.

Even your body is under the sway of Allah, Who created you. All of your organs and veins, as well as your nervous system and cells, are works of our Lord's superior wisdom and intelligence. None of the things were desired by you and then brought into existence by you. Once you opened your eyes to this world, you saw both the flawless system in your body and in the universe. However, you did not have any of them before, and you could not have acquired them through your own will in the latter part of your life. This fact surely holds true for all human beings. This being the case, Allah is the Lord and Creator of everything.

Despite this obvious fact, some people disregard all of these and, ignoring Allah's clear existence, assume that they own all of these things. Despite all of our weaknesses, along with their feelings of superiority, they grow arrogant and attempt to deny our Creator.

However, this denial only harms them, because as Prophet Musa (as) said: **"If you were to be ungrateful, you and everyone on Earth, Allah is Rich Beyond Need, Praiseworthy."** (Surah Ibrahim, 14:8)

AL-MAJEED
The Most Glorious One

The Possessor of the Throne, **the All-Glorious**. (Surat al-Buruj, 85:15)

Allah's glory manifests itself in every corner of the universe. All people recognize Allah's Highness, even those who deny Him or say: "We disbelieve," are, in actuality, well aware of His power and glory, for they witness His creation all around them. However, due to their arrogance, they do not believe.

The universe's glorious beauties and flawless systems also befit His glory. Clouds that carry tons of water in the sky, stars that are millions of light years away from us, waterfalls that fall with an enormous noise and intensity, unbounded oceans, mountains with snowy summits extending high into the sky, woods that are inhabited by living beings of countless colors, and noises are only a few of the beauties created by Allah.

An earthquake that razes a region in a few seconds, a volcanic eruption burying a city under a storm of hot lava, a hurricane causing extensive damage to the region it strikes, a devastating flood, a fatal lightning flash, a hurricane raging over cities, a flood ravaging populated areas, or a tornado sweeping away homes also are signs of Allah's power. These are only a very few signs showing Allah's power. As the Qur'an states:

He—exalted be the Majesty of our Lord!—has neither wife nor son. (Surat al-Jinn, 72:3)

They said: "Are you astonished at Allah's command? May Allah's mercy and His blessings be upon you, People of the House! He is Praiseworthy, All-Glorious." (Surah Hud, 11:73)

AL-MALJA
The Refuge

… and also toward the three who were left behind, so that when the land became narrow for them, for all its great breadth, and their own selves became constricted for them and **they realized that there was no refuge from Allah except in Him**, He turned to them so that they might turn to Him. Allah is the Ever-Returning, the Most Merciful. (Surat at-Tawba, 9:118)

All people are in need of prayer. A person who prays simply refers the situation to Allah, the Creator and Lord of the universe, and takes refuge in Him. Being aware that the solution lies only with Allah, the Almighty, taking Him as a friend and taking refuge in Him are great sources of security for His servants.

This taking refuge displays our weakness, for each of us has only limited power and will live only for a while. Therefore, we are obliged to seek His help. Allah, Who created us from a drop of water and the entire universe from nothing, can easily meet our needs and remove any problems. Other than Him, there is no being or thing in which to take refuge. Whoever is in the heavens or on Earth seeks His help. Those things or people from which people seek help and guidance cannot even help themselves. As Allah reveals:

O mankind! An example has been given, so listen carefully. Those whom you call upon besides Allah cannot even create a single fly, even if they were to join together to do it. And if a fly steals something from them, they cannot get it back. How feeble are both the seeker and the sought! (Surat al-Hajj, 22:73)

In the face of a threat or danger, all people understand that there is no one in whom to take refuge except for Allah. This is stated in the Qur'an, as follows:

> Say: "Who rescues you from the darkness of the land and sea? You call on Him humbly and secretly: "If you rescue us from this, we will truly be among the thankful.'" (Surat al-An'am, 6:63)

That people think only of Allah in times of hardship indicates that we innately know that Allah is our only true refuge. This being the case, we should take refuge in Allah before it is too late:

> Respond to your Lord before a Day comes from Allah that cannot be turned back. On that Day, you will have no hiding place and no means of denial. (Surat ash-Shura, 42:47)

AL-MALIK
The Sovereign; The King

Say: "I seek refuge with the Lord of mankind, **the King of mankind**, the God of mankind." (Surat an-Nas, 114:1-3)

The attribute *al-Malik* means that Allah is the sovereign of everything that exists, the Creator and sole Owner of all known and unknown universes, and the everlasting Sovereign of our universe. All stars, human beings, animals, plants, jinn, angels, demons, and other beings of which we are either aware or unaware are all under Allah's command. Allah, the Lord of all universes, also owns countless universes and regulates their amazing order.

It is unlikely that people who consciously submit to Almighty Allah considers themselves to be aimless beings. Allah is aware of everything, for He sees and hears everything. People who are aware of this also have to be aware that they are responsible to our Creator. Indeed, the consciousness that the universe's all-pervasive order has a unique owner makes believers naturally turn to Allah, Who holds sway over everything and everyone. Below are some of the verses related to this issue:

High exalted be Allah, the King, the Real!... (Surah Ta Ha, 20:114)

Exalted be Allah, the King, the Real. There is no deity but Him, Lord of the Noble Throne. (Surat al-Mu'minun, 23:116)

He is Allah—there is no deity but Him. He is the King, the Most Pure, the Perfect Peace, the Trustworthy, the Safeguarder, the Almighty, the Compeller, the Supremely

Great. Glory be to Allah above all they associate with Him. (Surat al-Hashr, 59:23)

AL-MATEEN
The Firm; The Possessor of Strength

Truly Allah, He is the Provider, **the Possessor of Strength**, the Sure. (Surat adh-Dhariyat, 51:58)

The issue that most misleads unbelievers is not Allah's existence, but His attributes. Some believe that Allah initially created everything and then left them to their own devices; others argue that although Allah created us, we do not have to feel any responsibility toward Him. To conclude, apart from denying Allah's existence, they do not measure Him with His true measure. This attitude underlies their unbelief, as **"They do not measure Allah with His true measure. Allah is All-Strong, Almighty"** (Surat al-Hajj, 22:74) reveals.

However, one day those who do not appreciate Allah's power, despite all of the surrounding evidence, will be unable to deny it. On that day, they will deeply feel Allah's power and strength. By His will, the strongest buildings and unshakable mountains will be crushed with a single blow:

So when the Trumpet is blown with a single blast, and the ground and the mountains are lifted and crushed with a single blow. On that Day, the Occurrence will occur and Heaven will be split apart, for that Day it will be very frail. (Surat al-Haqqa, 69:13-16)

The resulting destruction will befit Allah's glory and power. Oceans, the greatest source of life, will become like boiling water and then burst into flame. All the beings and orders with which humanity is accustomed will be demolished. The heavens and Earth will be crushed by the Power that created them. The sun, the source of energy that emitted light for millions of years, will become dull, thereby revealing that it has a master. Through these events, Allah will reveal that He is the sole and real Master, the only being having true sovereignty and power. One verse reads:

They do not measure Allah with His true measure. The whole Earth will be a mere handful for Him on the Day of Rising, the heavens folded up in His right hand. Glory be to Him! He is exalted above the partners they ascribe! (Surat az-Zumar, 39:67)

Through these events on the Day of Judgment, our Lord will show His power to all people. Those who insisted upon unbelief will finally comprehend His infinite power. But believers, as a reward for seeking His good pleasure throughout their lives, will meet His mercy. The Qur'an describes their joy on that Day in the following terms:

That Day some faces will be radiant, laughing, rejoicing. (Surah 'Abasa, 80:38-39)

AL-MAWLA
The Protector, The Master

No, **Allah is your Protector**. And He is the best of helpers. (Surah Al 'Imran, 3:150)

A believer knows that everyone and everything owes its existence to Allah, the Master of the Kingdom, for He sustains all beings and can end their existence at any time He wills. For this reason, Allah is a believer's sole friend and the only One Who can keep him or her far from sorrow or trouble. After all, our Lord's help and support is always with each believer. In return for this attitude, Allah sends down His serenity. (Surat at-Tawba, 9:26)

Several factors account for this serenity, among them is the believers' awareness that Allah hears every prayer, knows every good deed performed to earn His good pleasure, and that He will reward all of them bountifully. Another source of this feeling of security is their awareness of Allah's support with invisible armies and angels, as proclaimed in: **"Everyone has a succession of angels in front of him and behind him, guarding him by Allah's command..."** (Surat ar-Ra'd, 13:11) This aside, believers know that they will triumph in their struggle carried out in Allah's way, are given the good news of Paradise, and that Allah does not place an unbearable burden upon their shoulders. Believing in destiny and that Allah directs all affairs, they put their trust only in Allah. In the Qur'an, Allah calls attention to this state of mind, as follows:

Say: "Nothing can happen to us except what Allah has ordained for us. He is Our Master. It is in Allah that the believers should put their trust." (Surat at-Tawba, 9:51)

No doubt, Allah's friendship bears no resemblance to the friendship among believers. The believer taken by Allah as an intimate friend attains the most superior blessings both in this world and the next. It is a great blessing that our Lord, the Creator of everything, takes a created being as a friend. In the Qur'an, Allah tells us the following:

> Strive for Allah with the struggle due to Him. He has selected you and not placed any constraint upon you in the religion—the religion of your forefather Ibrahim. He named you Muslims before and also in this, so that the Messenger could be witness against you and you could be witnesses against all mankind. So perform prayer, pay alms, and hold fast to Allah. He is your Protector—the Best Protector, the Best Helper. (Surat al-Hajj, 22:78)

> Our Lord, do not take us to task if we forget or make a mistake. Our Lord, do not place on us a load like the one You placed on those before us. Our Lord, do not place on us a load we have not the strength to bear. Pardon us, forgive us, and have mercy upon us. You are our Master, so help us against the unbelievers. (Surat al-Baqara, 2:286)

> But if they turn away, know that Allah is your Master, the Best of Masters, and the Best of Helpers! (Surat al-Anfal, 8:40)

AL-MU' AKHKHIR / AL-MUQADDEEM
The Deferrer, The Keeper Behind
The Advancer

If Allah were to punish people for their wrong actions, not a single creature would be left upon Earth. But **He defers them until a predetermined time.** When their specified time arrives, they cannot delay it for a single hour or bring it forward. (Surat an-Nahl, 16:61)

Allah leaves behind and brings forward whoever He wills. Being the sole Creator of everything, He has the power to do whatever He wills with anything that exists. He determines the time for every event and, as the actual master of every being and its destiny, predetermines the events of every being's life. When the specified time arrives, what has been ordained takes place, according to His will. Allah calls attention to this fact in the Qur'an, as follows:

> **Every nation has an appointed time. When their time comes, they cannot delay it a single hour or bring it forward. (Surat al-A'raf, 7:34)**

No one except Allah knows this appointed time. No leaf falls before its appointed time, and every moment of a living being's life, from its birth to its death, is subject to this divine timing. However, if Allah wills, He can delay or bring forward any event, for the human concept of time being divided into the past, present, and future does not apply to Him. As the Qur'an states:

> **Do not consider Allah to be unaware of what the wrongdoers perpetrate. He is merely deferring them to a Day on which their sight will be transfixed. (Surat Ibrahim, 14:42)**

No nation can advance its appointed time, nor can they delay it. (Surat al-Hijr, 15:5)

This being the case, all sincere servants must strive to draw closer to Him, without considering what He has delayed or brought forward, and must be absolutely pleased with what He gives, for, as the verse maintains, **"Man is prone to be impetuous..."** (Surat al-Isra', 17:11) We often expect something to take place or to be over at once. Yet, only Allah knows what is best for us and so ordains all events and situations accordingly. What a person thinks might be good may actually be harmful. Thus, a believer should be pleased with whatever Allah ordains.

AL-MU'ADHDHIB
The Punisher

That Day, **no one will punish as He punishes** and no one will shackle as He shackles. (Surat al-Fajr, 89:25-26)

Despite all of the surrounding evidence, those who have no faith in Allah and who insist upon disregarding His grandeur and power surely deserve a great punishment, for Allah created us, placed us on Earth, and provided us with whatever we need. However, despite all of these blessings, some people insist on denial and even hate believers and try to destroy their faith. No doubt, such people will be repaid both in this world and beyond.

Allah directs some affairs in this world through His Messengers and sometimes punishes unbelievers in this world through the hands of His Messengers. Allah reveals this fact in the Qur'an, as follows:

If the hypocrites and those with a sickness in their hearts and the rumor-mongers in Madina do not desist, We will set you upon them. Then they will only be your neighbors there for a very short time. They are an accursed people. Wherever they are found, they should be seized and mercilessly put to death. This is Allāh's pattern with those who passed away before. You will not find any alteration in Allah's pattern. (Surat al-Ahzab, 33:60-62)

Their fearsome punishment in the Hereafter will continue to exist, unless Allah wills otherwise, for all eternity. Allah created various forms of psychological and physical punishments, for He knows each person's most secret weaknesses. Thus, He is the One Who can give the most suitable punishment. According to the following verses:

But as for those who do not believe in the Hereafter, We have prepared for them a painful punishment. (Surat al-Isra', 17:10)

But as for those who are deviators, their refuge is the Fire. Every time that they want to get out, they are put straight back into it again and are told: "Taste the punishment of the Fire, which you denied." We will give them a taste of lesser punishment before the greater punishment, so that hopefully they will turn back. (Surat as-Sajda, 32:20-21)

Tell My servants that I am the Ever-Forgiving, the Most Merciful, but also that My punishment is the Painful Punishment. (Surat al-Hijr, 15:49-50)

Those before them also plotted, and Allah came at their building from the foundations and the roof caved in on top of them. The punishment came at them from where they did not expect. (Surat an-Nahl, 16:26)

As for those who were unbelievers and barred access to the way of Allah, We will heap punishment on top of their punishment because of the corruption they brought about. (Surat an-Nahl, 16:88)

However, we need to remember that Allah creates infinite opportunities for each of us to repent and take refuge in His mercy. When we turn to Him in sincere repentance we will find our Lord to be the most merciful and compassionate, regardless of what type of sins one has committed. Allah gives the good news of His infinite mercy to His servants who sincerely repent:

But if anyone repents after his wrongdoing and puts things right, Allah will turn toward him. Allah is Ever-Forgiving, Most Merciful. (Surat al-Ma'ida, 5:39)

But I am Ever-Forgiving to anyone who repents, believes, acts rightly, and then is guided. (Surah Ta Ha, 20:82)

AL-MUHEET
All-Pervading; The All-Encompassing

What! Are they in doubt about the meeting with their Lord? What! **Does He not encompass all things?** (Surah Fussilat, 41:54)

People who are far from religion assume that believers do not notice their forgeries and lies, a false assumption that gradually causes them to become arrogant. Yet, all of their forgeries are against themselves, even though they do not perceive this fact. At this point, they make another serious mistake: They fail to realize that Allah, Who witnesses, sees and hears everything, is all around them at all times. As the Qur'an reveals:

They try to conceal themselves from people, but they cannot conceal themselves from Allah. He is with them when they spend the night saying things that are not pleasing to Him. Allah encompasses everything they do. (Surat an-Nisa', 4:108)

Not a thought or whisper remains hidden from Allah. He knows everyone's most secret secrets, for He is nearer to them than their jugular veins. And, as He encompasses the entire universe, He controls all beings. This is true even for those universes of which we know very little or nothing, such as the realms of the angels, jinn, and many others. Allah calls attention to this fact in the following verse:

If something good happens to you, it galls them. If something bad strikes you, they rejoice at it. But if you are steadfast and guard against evil, their scheming will not harm you in any way. Allah encompasses what they do. (Surah Al 'Imran, 3:120)

AL-MUDHHEEK / AL-MUBKI
He Who Brings about both Laughter and Tears

That it is He Who brings about both laughter and tears. (Surat an-Najm, 53:43)

Believers know that Allah creates whatever they experience and thus are pleased with Him in all circumstances, no matter how difficult. Knowing that mundane things are transitory, they do not grieve over any loss, for they know that their moral excellence will be fully rewarded in the Hereafter. Moreover, Allah promises believers the best life in this world.

This is surely not the case with unbelievers, who pursue only this life in the belief that they are fully independent from Allah. This mistaken belief, however, causes them to feel great pressure upon their souls. Constantly seeking to earn other peoples' approval and attain mundane goals makes them afraid and confused, for such attitudes force them to think about everything and consider every possibility. But human beings, who are feeble, cannot shoulder such a burden, for the human body and soul were created to put trust and faith in Allah. Indeed, this delusion is the cause of their wailing, grief, and trouble, for such people wrong themselves by turning away from Allah. Allah relates how He will repay them both in this world and the next, as follows:

Let them laugh little and weep much, in repayment for what they have earned. (Surat at-Tawba, 9:82)

Allah punishes unbelievers through every incident and reason that causes them to weep. Meanwhile, He gives joy, happiness, peace, and tranquility to His believing servants, and makes them laugh constantly. He removes their sadness, for He is their friend and helper. Even if they face hardship and trouble, He gives them patience and strength and never causes them to despair. Believers only weep in prostration, over the awe they feel for our Lord's grandeur. Destined to have joy both in this world and the next, they experience the contentment related in the following verses:

> **As for those who believed and did right actions, they will be made joyful in a verdant meadow. (Surat ar-Rum, 30:15)**
>
> **The Companions of the Garden are busy enjoying themselves today. (Surah Ya Sin, 36:55)**
>
> **"My servants, you will feel no fear today; you will know no sorrow." As for those who believed in Our Signs and became Muslims: "Enter the Garden, you and your spouses, delighting in your joy." (Surat az-Zukhruf, 43:68-70)**
>
> **The people who have consciousness of Allah will be in Gardens of Delight, savoring what their Lord has given them. Their Lord will safeguard them from the punishment of the Blazing Fire. (Surat at-Tur, 52:17-18)**

In the Hereafter, unbelievers and believers will be recognized and separated by their facial expressions. This distinction is described below, as follows:

> **That Day some faces will be radiant, laughing, rejoicing. That Day some faces will be dust-covered, overcast with gloom. Those are the dissolute unbelievers. (Surah 'Abasa, 80:38-42)**

AL-MUWAFFEE
He Who Keeps His Word, He Who Pays in Full

So be in no doubt about what these people worship. They only worship as their ancestors worshipped previously. **We will pay them their portion in full, with no rebate!** (Surah Hud, 11:109)

All of our acts and thoughts are recorded in Allah's Sight. He forgets nothing, even the most insignificant detail. Since "**... even if something weighs as little as a mustard-seed and is inside a rock or anywhere else in the heavens or earth, Allah will bring it out. Allah is All-Pervading, All-Aware**" (Surah Luqman, 31:16), on the Day of Judgment each of us will see our acts, as recorded upon their Pages, and will be repaid accordingly. Allah relates the following fact:

> **That Day, people will emerge segregated to see the results of their actions. Whoever does an atom's weight of good will see it. Whoever does an atom's weight of evil will see it. (Surat az-Zilzal, 99:6-8)**

On that Day, all of a person's acts will be weighed in balances specially prepared for the Day of Judgment. In the face of Allah's Justice, no one will be wronged in any way:

> **We will set up the Just Balance on the Day of Rising, and no self will be wronged in any way. Even if it is no more than the weight of a grain of mustard-seed, We will produce it. We are sufficient as a Reckoner. (Surat al-Anbiya', 21:47)**

Every act will be weighed to determine one's reward, for:

As for him whose balance is heavy, he will have a most pleasant life. But as for him whose balance is light, his motherland is Hawiya. And what will convey to you what that is? A raging Fire! (Surat al-Qari'a, 101:6-11)

Allah's justice demands that everyone receive full payment for what they have done. Allah's repayment according to people's prayers and acts also takes place in this world. While this is a great blessing for believers, it is a fearsome trap for unbelievers, who do not realize the enormity of their spiritual blindness, for:

As for those who desire the life of the world and its finery, We will give them full payment in it for their actions. They will not be deprived here of their due. But such people will have nothing in the Hereafter but the Fire. What they achieved here will come to nothing. What they did will prove to be null and void. (Surah Hud, 11:15-16)

AL-MUHSEE
The Reckoner

He has counted them and numbered them precisely. (Surat al-Maryam, 19:94)

As Allah informs us in **"Does He Who created not then know?"** (Surat al-Mulk, 67:14), He knows even the most delicate features of all members of creation. In fact, He holds them all by their forelocks, for He created their colors, shapes, images, and features, and also determined their number. Surely, no person can ever possess this knowledge.

Allah knows the number of planets, stars, and celestial bodies, as well as the number of electrons circling an atom's nucleus, how many leaves exist on trees, and the number of atoms in each leaf. In addition, He knows the exact number of sand grains located on and below Earth's surface, the number of rain drops, and how many fish live in the oceans. Given that He created everything, He also knows the exact number of animal and plant species on Earth, the precise number of people who have lived since the time of Prophet Adam (as), and the number of people who will live until the Day of Judgment.

Given His comprehensive knowledge, the Qur'an relates the following fact:

> On the Day Allah raises up all of them together, He will inform them of what they did. Allah has recorded it, while they have forgotten it. Allah is a Witness of all things. (Surat al-Mujadala, 58:6)

AL-MUHSIN
The Giver

Say: "**All favor is in Allah's Hand, and He gives it to whoever He wills**. Allah is All-Encompassing, All-Knowing. He picks out for His mercy whoever He wills. **Allah's favor is indeed immense**." (Surah Al 'Imran, 3:73-74)

One of Allah's immutable laws is that He rewards His sincere servants, both for their zeal and as an indication of His favor, with blessings and beauty. Since wealth, glory, and beauty are the basic attributes of Paradise, Allah creates similar settings and blessings to remind His beloved servants of Paradise and to augment their desire and excitement for it. That is why, just as unbelievers' infinite punishment starts in this world, Allah starts presenting the infinite beauties He promises to His sincere believers in this world.

In one verse, Allah states that He will grant those who repent and seek His forgiveness blessings also in this world. One verse reads:

Ask your Lord for forgiveness and then repent to Him. He will let you enjoy a good life until a specified time, and will give His favor to all who merit it. But if you turn your backs, I fear for you the punishment of a Mighty Day. (Surah Hud, 11:3)

Believers always meet Allah's favor and help. Being aware of the grandeur of Almighty Allah, Who created them, they comply with His commands and prohibitions, live by the religion with which He is pleased, and, most importantly, have great hopes and expectations for their next life. Allah will recompense them for the best of what they did, for He rewards every good made for His cause, as the following verses proclaim:

> Will the reward for doing good be anything other than good? (Surat ar-Rahman, 55:60)

> What will those who invent lies against Allah think on the Day of Rising? Allah shows favor to mankind, but most of them are not thankful. (Surah Yunus, 10:60)

> Nor will they give away any amount, whether large or small; nor will they cross any valley, without it being written down for them, so that Allah can recompense them for the best of what they did. (Surat at-Tawba, 9:121)

> The metaphor of those who spend their wealth in the Way of Allah is that of a grain that produces seven ears; in every ear are a hundred grains. Allah gives such multiplied increase to whoever He wills. Allah is All-Encompassing, All-Knowing. (Surat al-Baqara, 2:261)

> Satan promises you poverty and commands you to avarice. Allah promises you forgiveness from Him and abundance. Allah is All-Encompassing, All-Knowing. (Surat al-Baqara, 2:268)

AL-MUHEE
The Giver of Life

He gives life and causes to die, and you will be returned to Him. (Surah Yunus, 10:56)

Giving life to all beings, creating them from nothing, and surrounding them with the proper conditions for their survival is a feature unique to Allah, Who has infinite power.

Allah makes a sperm unite an ovum, both of which are invisible to the naked eye. As soon as the sperm destined to fertilize the egg enters the ovum, a membrane covers the egg and a new life begins. Allah divides this tiny cell first into two and then into four. This process proceeds rapidly, and the end result is a miraculous life starting in the mother's womb. After some time, these cells change in order to form the embryo's brain, nervous system, bones, and cartilage. This way, within only 9 months, Allah creates from nothing a human being who sees, hears, speaks, and uses his or her intelligence. He then grants life. Obviously, an egg and a sperm cannot accomplish these series of miraculous events, for only Allah causes them to unite and then protects the embryo within the mother's womb for nine months. This is the first creation and the first bringing to life.

Allah grants life to each human being and destines each one to die on a particular day. Until then, He tests them in the life of this world. At the appointed time, He takes their lives and, on the Day of Judgment, resurrects them, just as He first created them from nothing, to repay them for what they did in the world. No doubt, this is easy for Allah, the Almighty. Yet those who ignore this resurrection say:

He makes likenesses of Us and forgets his own creation, saying: "Who will give life to bones when they are decayed?" (Surah Ya Sin, 36:78)

Allah promises that the Resurrection will occur, as the following verses indicate:

Say: "He Who made them in the first place will bring them back to life. He has total knowledge of each created thing." (Surah Ya Sin, 36:79)

So look at the effect of Allah's mercy, how He brings the dead earth back to life. Truly He brings the dead to life. He has power over all things. (Surat ar-Rum, 30:50)

Among His Signs is that you see the earth laid bare, and then, when We send down water on it, it quivers and swells. He Who gives it life also gives life to the dead. Certainly He has power over all things. (Surah Fussilat, 41:39)

AL-MUQALLIB
The Turner of People's Hearts

We will overturn their hearts and sight, just as when they did not believe in it at first, and We will abandon them to wander blindly in their excessive insolence. (Surat al-An'am, 6:110)

We cannot know Allah and grasp the purpose of our existence if we lack knowledge about the religion with which He is pleased. Moreover, we cannot understand the divine purposes behind the creation of the universe and its countless inhabitants, life, death, the Hereafter, Paradise, Hell, angels, and Satan on our own. Many people live and die in heedlessness. However, if Allah places faith in our hearts, we find all of the answers to these questions. Allah then purifies our hearts and makes us sincere toward the religion. A person who used to be hostile to religion starts to be positive toward religion; one who used to ignore His commands begins to adhere to them meticulously and remembers Him continuously. Likewise, they start to thank Allah frequently for the blessings that they have received. Whereas before they disregarded the signs of Allah's existence, as well as His favors, mercy, and compassion, they now recognize all of these. In brief, sincere believers are like those people who wake up from sleep, for Allah moves them from unbelief to belief by placing faith in their hearts.

Just as Allah grants faith, He can remove it whenever He wills. Having faith depends upon remembering Allah, for only a heart that submits itself to Allah can find guidance. Unbelievers, lost in their delusions, cannot see or recognize the clear signs of Allah's existence all around them. In many verses, Allah states that such people's hearts are covered in such a way that they cannot grasp the truth:

> Who could do greater wrong than someone who is reminded of the Signs of his Lord and then turns away from them, forgetting all that he has done before? We have placed covers on their hearts, preventing them from understanding it, and heaviness in their ears. Though you call them to guidance, they will nonetheless never be guided. (Surat al-Kahf, 18:57)

Unbelievers sometimes admit that they cannot understand religion's message. The people of Prophet Shu'ayb (as) is a clear example:

> They said: "Shu'ayb, We do not understand much of what you say, and we see that you are weak among us..." (Surah Hud, 11:91)

If one's heart is veiled and Allah hinders comprehension, then they can never be guided unless Allah wills otherwise. Allah calls attention to this, as follows:

> Among them there are some who listen to you. But can you make the deaf hear, even though they cannot understand? Among them there are some who look at you. But can you guide the blind, even though they cannot see? (Surah Yunus, 10:42-43)

Allah causes the heart of those who desire faith and closeness to Him to yield to His remembrance and unites them with other Muslims. Meanwhile, He turns the hearts of those who are insincere toward unbelief. He has the power to turn the heart of anyone He wills at any time, and no one can change a heart that Allah has covered.

AL-MUKMIL
He Who Perfects

Today the unbelievers have despaired of overcoming your religion. So do not be afraid of them, but be afraid of Me. **Today I have perfected your religion** for you and completed My blessing upon you, and I am pleased with Islam as a religion for you. But if anyone is forced by hunger, not intending any wrongdoing, Allah is Ever-Forgiving, Most Merciful. (Surat al-Ma'ida, 5:3)

Allah created humanity and, as **"Does He Who created not then know? He is the All-Pervading, the All-Aware"** (Surat al-Mulk, 67:14) emphasizes, He knows best what we need. Allah presented the religion in the form that best conforms to our nature so that all of us could know and serve Him, and thereby attain eternal happiness and salvation. Our Lord, the All-Wise, is pleased with Islam. No doubt, only Allah perfects the religion and uses it, in turn, to perfect His servants.

AL-MUQTADIR
The Powerful

Make a metaphor for them of the life of the world. It is like water that We send down from the sky and the plants of the earth combine with it, but then become dry chaff scattered by the winds. **Allah has absolute power over everything.** (Surat al-Kahf, 18:45)

Allah granted unprecedented power and possessions to some people of the past. He gave them authority to administer their lands, and made them leaders of their people. One of these people was Pharaoh, who grew arrogant and assumed that this power belonged to him to such an extent that he proclaimed himself a deity. This is related in the following verse:

Pharaoh said: "Council, I do not know of any other deity for you apart from Me..." (Surat al-Qasas, 28:38)

Pharaoh called to his people, saying: "My people, does the kingdom of Egypt not belong to me? Do not all of these rivers flow under my control?..." (Surat az-Zukhruf, 43:51)

Upon this arrogance, All-Mighty Allah drowned both him and his army:

He and his troops were arrogant in the land, without any right. They thought that they would not return to Us. So, We seized him and his troops and flung them into the sea. See the final fate of the wrongdoers! (Surat al-Qasas, 28:39-40)

Haman and Qarun were destined for the same end, for they had become insolent and arrogant due to their armies and possessions. However, Allah showed them Who was the real owner of power, as follows:

> And Qarun and Pharaoh and Haman—Musa came with the Clear Signs to them, but they were arrogant in the land. They could not outstrip Us. We seized each one of them for their wrong actions. Against some We sent a sudden squall of stones, some of them were seized by the Great Blast, some We caused the ground to swallow up, and some We drowned. Allah did not wrong them; rather, they wronged themselves. (Surat al-'Ankabut, 29:39-40)

Pharaoh did not realize several facts: Only Allah has real power and authority; grants people's possessions, authority, and armies; makes the Sun rise every day and covers the day with night; holds the fast-moving planets in their orbits; and controls all of the countless orders in the universe. Once people lose their authority and possessions, they lose their strength. When they lose their health, they become weak and feeble. Through such events, Allah shows His servants Who has real power. As the Qur'an proclaims:

> They dismissed every one of Our Signs, and so We seized them with the seizing of One Who is Almighty, All-Powerful. (Surat al-Qamar, 54:42)

> Or let you see what We have promised them. They are completely in Our power. (Surat az-Zukhruf, 43:42)

AL-MUNTAQIM
The Retaliator

Then when they had provoked Our wrath, **We inflicted Our retribution** on them and drowned every one of them. (Surat az- Zukhruf, 43:55)

Allah warns every nation through His chosen Messengers so that they might be saved from idolatry and degeneration. As for those who ignore these warnings and grow more insolent, Allah punishes them. And, His retribution is surely unlike that of people:
Those who did not believe will be addressed: "Allah's abhorrence of you, when you were called to faith but then chose unbelief, is even greater than your hatred of yourselves." (Surat al-Ghafir, 40:10)
In most cases, Allah may delay His punishment upon those people who were warned, and thus were informed of the truth, to give them more time to acquire faith and purify themselves. However, the majority of people use this time to strengthen their existing insolence. Therefore, they deserve a humiliating punishment. As Allah states:
It is coming closer to you and closer. Then closer to you and closer still. Does man reckon that he will be left to go on unchecked? (Surat al-Qiyama, 75:34-36)
According to the Qur'an, denying our Lord, being insolent and ungrateful toward Him, and refusing to abandon such defiant attitudes are among the greatest crimes that a person can commit. This is why Allah punishes unbelievers in ways that they could never have imagined. In one verse, Allah informs us that He is the

Retaliator:

On the day We launch the Great Assault, We will certainly inflict Our retribution. (Surat ad-Dukhan, 44:16)

This aside, many verses speak of Allah's infinite compassion and the manifestations of His attributes of *al-Rahman* and *al-Raheem*. The punishments waiting for unbelievers in the Hereafter are the result of their resolute unbelief. Allah reminds people of this fact and informs them that He does not wrong them, as follows:

[Angels will say to unbelievers:] "That is for what you did. Allah does not wrong His servants." (Surat al-Anfal, 8:51)

Allah would not punish them while you were among them. Allah would not punish them as long as they sought forgiveness. (Surat al-Anfal, 8:33)

These are Allah's Signs, which We recite to you with truth. Allah desires no wrong for any being. (Surah Al 'Imran, 3:108)

Our Lord, Who is Most Merciful, also relates that He intends to lead all of His servants to the right path and to perfect His blessings upon them, as follows:

Allah desires to make things clear to you, to guide you to the correct practices of those before you, and to turn toward you. Allah is All-Knowing, All-Wise. (Surat an-Nisa', 4:26)

Allah does not want to make things difficult for you; rather, ... He wants to purify you and perfect His blessing upon you so that hopefully you will be thankful. (Surat al-Ma'ida, 5:6)

AL-MUSAWWIR
The Shaper; The Giver of Form

He is Allah—the Creator, the Maker, **the Giver of Form**. To Him belong the Most Beautiful Names. Everything in the heavens and Earth glorifies Him. He is the Almighty, the All-Wise. (Surat al-Hashr, 59:24)

Our planet contains thousands of different species with entirely different appearances and amazing features. Let's examine the flawless symmetry on a butterfly wing. The surface of each wing is embellished with different patterns and impressive colors. No matter how complicated these patterns and colors may be, they never harm the perfect symmetry between the two wings. Indeed, just like a painter's masterpiece, all butterflies have astonishing appearances. Clearly, the wisdom manifested in such beauty has a source, for even an ordinary painting is painted by someone; it could not have come into existence by itself. This being the case, how could such a perfect living being, one that is as aesthetic as a work of art, come into being by coincidence? Allah, Lord of the universe, created, designed, and formed all of those beings.

Allah, Who created human beings and designed their bodies' internal and external systems, manifests His superior creativity and power on every detail of this complex structure. For instance, the skeleton (the body's structural support system) is an engineering marvel in its own right. It protects such vital organs as the brain, the heart and lungs, and upholds the body's internal organs. In addition, it gives the body a superior capacity for movement, one that cannot be imitated by any artificial mechanism. Bone tissue is not inorganic, as many people think. In fact, it is the body's mineral bank and thus includes many important minerals, among them calcium and phosphate. In accordance with the body's needs, it either stores these minerals or delivers them to where they are needed. Moreover, bones also produce red blood cells. Yet this multi-functional system is only one of the perfect systems existing in the human body.

This is the way of Allah, Who created—and Who continues to create—all of these systems with an unparalleled design so that we may see wherever we turn the manifestations of His unique creation. One verse relates that believers say the following words:

... **"Our Lord gives each thing its created form and then guides it." (Surah Ta Ha, 20:50)**

AL-MUBASHSHIR
The Giver Of Good News

That is the good news that Allah gives to His servants who believe and do right actions. Say: "I do not ask you for any wage for this—except for you to love your near of kin. If anyone does a good action, We will increase the good of it for him. Allah is Ever-Forgiving, Ever-Thankful." (Surat ash-Shura, 42:23)

Sincere believers who display the attributes mentioned in the Qur'an, who remain loyal to Allah's religion, and who do not associate partners with Him are given the good news of rewards both in this world and in the next. For example:

Their Lord gives them the good news of His mercy and good pleasure, and of gardens where they will enjoy everlasting delight. (Surat at-Tawba, 9:21)

There is good news for them in the life of the world and in the Hereafter. There is no changing the words of Allah. That is the great victory! (Surah Yunus, 10:64)

The angels descend on those who say: "Our Lord is Allah," and then go straight: "Do not fear and do not grieve, but rejoice in the garden you have been promised. We are your protectors in the life of the world and the Hereafter. You will have there all that you could wish for. You will have there everything you demand. Hospitality from One Who is Ever-Forgiving, Most Merciful." (Surah Fussilat, 41:30-32)

Apart from the good news of Paradise, the source of eternal

happiness and joy, Allah gives many glad tidings to His sincere servants in this world as well. He proclaims these glad tidings in the Qur'an and describes how He answers prayers. For example, Allah told the Prophets that those nations who are insolent toward them would be destroyed. Similarly, He answered the prayers of those Prophets for sons. He gave Prophet Zakariyya (as) the good news of Prophet Yahya (as). Similarly, Maryam was given the good news of Prophet 'Isa (as), and Prophet Ibrahim (as) was given the good news of Prophet Ishaq (as) and Prophet Ya'qub (as). The related verses read:

"O Zakariyya. We give you the good news of a boy named Yahya, a name we have given to no one else before." (Surah Maryam, 19:7)

And We gave him the good news of a forbearing boy. (Surat as-Saffat, 37:101)

AL-MUBAYYIN
The One Who Makes His Signs Clear

In this way **Allah makes His Signs clear to you**, so that hopefully you will use your intellect. (Surat al-Baqara, 2:242)

Given that Allah has explained, through His Messengers and His revelation why we were created, what we have to accomplish, and what we will go through after death, we cannot claim ignorance of these facts. If He had not done so, we would exist in a state of helplessness, feebleness, and fear. But Allah, Who is compassionate and merciful toward His servants, answers all of our questions through His revelations. In this way, He brings people to life. Indeed, the calls, warnings, recommendations, and prohibitions revealed by Him, as well as the issues to which He draws people's attention, are for our salvation and will enable us to give a joyful account in Allah's presence on the Day of Judgment.

Almighty Allah, Who doesn't want any injustice for His servants, gives a detailed account of how they can avoid eternal punishment and all they need to know to serve Him. In addition, He gives them examples of earlier peoples so that they will not repeat their ancestors' mistakes, and tells them about the Prophets so that they can find the right path. Indeed, people could never learn about such events and conversations on their own. For instance, no one witnessed Prophet Musa's (as) conversation with Allah in the valley of Tuwa, and there is no record of it. But Allah lets us know some details of this conversation. Thus, His words to Prophet Musa (as), even though they were spoken before no one else and were uttered centuries ago, are conveyed to everyone word by word.

You were not on the western side when We gave Musa the command. You were not a witness. Yet We produced further generations and ages passed. Nor did you live among the people of Madyan and recite Our Signs to them, yet We have sent you news of them. Nor were you on the side of the Mount when We called, yet it is a mercy from your Lord so that you can warn a people to whom no warner came before, so that hopefully they will pay heed. (Surat al-Qasas, 28:44-46)

In addition, no other book informs people about the life of the Hereafter. The Qur'an informs us that there is a life after death and that this worldly life is only a preparation for the Hereafter. In the absence of such knowledge, people would have to be content with the information relating to this world and would have no idea about the life after death. These are only a few issues that Allah explains to His servants. Through the Qur'an, our Lord provides people with everything that they need to know. One verse reads:

There is instruction in their stories for people of intelligence. This is not a narration that has been invented, but a confirmation of all that came before, a clarification of everything, a guidance and a mercy for people who believe. (Surah Yusuf, 12:111)

We have no knowledge other than what is revealed to us by our Lord.

AL-MUDABBIR
The Ruler, the Director, Who governs all of creation with order and balance

Your Lord is Allah, Who created the heavens and Earth in six days and then established Himself firmly on the Throne. **He directs the whole affair**... (Surah Yunus, 10:3)

Allah holds sway over the entire universe, for not a single atom moves without Him knowing it. Allah is the sole ruler of everything, from a dust particle to the planets following their orbits to the billions of inhabitants living in the micro-universe. The sky that serves as a dome by His grace, the billions of stars, the planets proceeding in their orbits, and the Sun have all submitted to Allah. This perfect order proves the existence of a power that controls all of existence, regardless of time or location. This power, which is over and above any other power, manifests Allah's perfect creation.

When we gaze at Earth, we encounter an amazing order. Allah assigns every living being a particular duty, and they carry out these duties fully. For instance, trees inhale carbon dioxide and exhale oxygen. The soil produces edible food, rain falls in due measure and at a particular rate, and after a lightning flash comes thunder. This balance is always maintained. While some people die, others are born.

Allah also rules the bodies of all living beings with great balance and order, for He has caused all organs to help one another. For instance, people cannot make their hearts beat or their intestines digest food. Nor can they be aware of the war waged by leucocytes in their blood against microbes, or of the countless chemical reactions taking place in their bodies. And, in no way can they supervise them.

In addition, human life relies on countless external factors that are ruled by Allah with great order and balance. If Allah had created the universe and then left it to its own devices, as some people claim, everything would have been ruined at that very moment. In fact, all of those interrelated systems have remained intact and continue to exist because of our Creator's power, for Allah is the real owner and ruler of the universe. The Qur'an calls attention to this fact, as follows:

Allah keeps a firm hold on the heavens and Earth, preventing them from vanishing. And if they vanished, no one could then keep hold of them. Certainly He is Lenient, Ever-Forgiving. (Surah Fatir, 35:41)

AL-MU'MIN
The Trustworthy, He Who Gives Tranquillity

He is Allah—there is no deity but Him. He is the King, the Most Pure, the Perfect Peace, **the Trustworthy**, the Safeguarder, the Almighty, the Compeller, the Supremely Great. Glory be to Allah above all that they associate with Him. (Surat al-Hashr, 59:23)

Allah presents a pleasing life to believers both in this world and the next. This life, which is perfect in all respects, makes them spiritually strong. Indeed, Allah gives spiritual peace and security to sincere believers. When they face any difficulty, He supports them, confirms His signs on their hearts, and, through the trust they put in Him, allows them to lead a peaceful life. The Qur'an informs us about this spiritual support after the Companions suffered a defeat during the time of our Prophet (saas):

Allah has helped you on many occasions, including the Day of Hunayn, when your great numbers delighted you but did not help you in any way, and the land seemed narrow to you for all its great breadth, and you turned your backs. Then Allah sent down His serenity on His Messenger and on the believers, and sent down troops you could not see, and punished those who were unbelievers. That is how the unbelievers are repaid. Then after that, Allah will turn to anyone He wills. Allah is Ever-Forgiving, Most Merciful. (Surat at-Tawba, 9:25-27)

There have always been people who, insisting upon denying Allah, work to turn sincere believers away from the straight path and to their own man-made religion. When believers reject this call, unbelievers threaten and oppress them. But during such times, Allah provides all forms of support and undermines the unbelievers' efforts, as the Qur'an reveals:

> Those who are disbelievers filled their hearts with fanatical rage—the fanatical rage of the Time of Ignorance—and Allah sent down serenity to His Messenger and to the believers, and bound them to the expression of heedfulness, to which they had most right and were most entitled. Allah has knowledge of all things. (Surat al-Fath, 48:26)

Many other verses inform us about this spiritual support, especially that given to the Messengers. When unbelievers forced our Prophet (saas) to emigrate, Allah promised to support him, hindered the unbelievers' attacks, and sent down serenity upon his heart. This support is related in the following verses:

> If you do not help him, Allah did help him when the unbelievers drove him out and there were two of them in the cave. He said to his companion: "Do not be despondent, Allah is with us." Then Allah sent down His serenity upon him and reinforced him with troops you could not see. He made the word of the unbelievers the lowest of the low. It is the word of Allah that is uppermost. Allah is Almighty, All-Wise. (Surat at-Tawba, 9:40)

While Allah gives His sincere servants feelings of security and serenity, the peace and security of the Hereafter are far beyond our comprehension. For one thing, they will last for all eternity, if Allah so wills. Allah describes this unique state of material and spiritual contentment, as follows:

> Those who guard against evil will be amid gardens and springs: "Enter them in peace, in complete security!" We

will strip away any rancor in their hearts—brothers [and sisters], resting on couches face-to-face. They will not be affected by any tiredness there and will never be made to leave. (Surat al-Hijr, 15:45-48)

AL-MUJEEB
The Answerer

If My servants ask you about Me, I am near. **I answer the call of the caller when he calls upon Me.** They should, therefore, respond to Me and believe in Me so that hopefully they will be rightly guided. (Surat al-Baqara, 2:186)

Prayer is an intimate and personal bond between people and Allah. Through prayer, people express all of their troubles and wishes to Allah and seek His help. In return, He hears His servants' calls and answers their prayers. He is closer to people than their jugular veins, knows and hears everything, and is fully aware of each inner thought. This being the case, even just thinking is enough to ask for something from Him. This shows how close Allah's answer is.

Believers are certain that Allah hears and answers their prayers in one way or another, for they know that Allah wills everything. For this reason, they never worry that their prayers will remain unanswered. Doubting Allah's answer means that one fails to appreciate His power. Allah answers each prayer with great ease. However, "answering a prayer" does not mean that the person receives an immediate answer or even the one that he or she is expecting. In one verse, Allah states:

Man prays for evil just as he prays for good. Man is prone to be impetuous. (Surat al-Isra', 17:11)

Allah knows best what is good and what is bad for us, for He is the One Who directs all affairs. As is in all of His acts, He answers prayers in the way that best meets His many divine purposes, as the

Qur'an reveals below:

Fighting is prescribed for you, even if it is hateful to you. It may be that you hate something when it is good for you, and it may be that you love something when it is bad for you. Allah knows, and you do not know. (Surat al-Baqara, 2:216)

Allah's answer to all prayers, whether hidden or open, manifests His glory. No thought or wish remains unanswered. And, only Allah hears and answers prayers, for:

Those you call on besides Allah are servants, just like yourselves. Call on them and let them respond to you, if you are telling the truth. (Surat al-A'raf, 7:194)

AL-MUHAYMIN
The Safeguarder, The Protector

He is Allah—there is no deity but Him. He is the King, the Most Pure, the Perfect Peace, the Trustworthy, **the Safeguarder**, the Almighty, the Compeller, the Supremely Great. Glory be to Allah above all they associate with Him. (Surat al-Hashr, 59:23)

The laws of physics, which ensure a flawless order in the universe, are the best evidence of the divine protection of Allah, Who created them, over His servants. For instance, what would happen if Earth's gravity were less? Primarily, light things would not remain fixed on Earth. In the mildest breeze, a dust or a sand particle would flit about for hours. The speed of rain drops would slow down, causing them to evaporate before falling on the ground. Newton's law of gravitation, which explains the delicate balance between the orbits of Earth, the Moon, and the planets, is another example. A minor change in this balance would cause Earth to draw near to the Sun and thus burn or be thrown into space, where it would freeze.

What would a world deprived of friction between objects and surfaces look like? A pen would slip out of one's hand, books and objects would slide down tables, and a table would slide and hit the wall. In brief, all objects would slide and roll. In a world without friction, all knots would unfasten, nails and screws would come out, brakes would never function, and sounds would continue to resound from one wall to another...

Another example is Earth's secure and strong structure. Toward its center, the temperature rises by 30° Celsius (86° Fahrenheit) every kilometer, reaching probably 4,500° Celsius (8,132° Fahrenheit) at its core. When we consider that only 1 kilometer (0,6214 miles) below the surface the temperature reaches 60° Celsius (140° Fahrenheit), we can grasp the dimensions of this threat. Despite this, however, all living beings lead their lives in absolute security, unaware of the magma boiling underneath them.

Clearly, Allah creates a perfect order on Earth's surface, which actually shelters an internal ball of fire. Thus, there is no room for any randomness. He holds sway over the heavens and Earth and protects all living beings in the universe against all threats, whether known to them or not. Meanwhile, He places the fetus in a very protected place. As these examples show, many things that seem normal to us are, in actuality, manifestations of His mercy and divine protection over His servants, for there is no other reason for the existence of such order and unity in the universe. Allah is the best of protectors.

AL-MUTA'ALEE
The All-Exalted

High exalted be Allah, the King, the Real! Do not rush ahead with the Qur'an before its revelation to you is complete, and say: "My Lord, increase me in knowledge." (Surah Ta Ha, 20:114)

Some people, despite the countless signs surrounding them, fail to appreciate Allah's greatness. Despite their helplessness, they grow arrogant and never think about our Creator, because they follow the urgings of their lower self, which encourages them to indulge in evil. Yet the faithful, aware of their helplessness before Allah's greatness, understand that they have no real power whatsoever. Allah calls attention to creation's helplessness and His greatness in the following example:

O mankind! An example has been made, so listen carefully. Those whom you call upon besides Allah cannot even create a single fly, even if they were to join together to do it. And if a fly steals something from them, they cannot get it back. How feeble are both the seeker and the sought! They do not measure Allah with His true measure. Allah is All-Strong, Almighty. (Surat al-Hajj, 22:73-74)

Even though every corner of the universe manifests Allah's greatness, this vast manifestation is not sufficient to explain His infinite power and greatness. Allah is exalted above any partnership, defects, and limits. He is the sole Owner of all beautiful names and superior attributes. His knowledge, wisdom, might, power, mercy, compassion, and generosity is infinite.

The word "infinite" is a concept over which one has to think a lot in order to grasp Allah's greatness. After death, Allah will create people anew and make them start a new life either in Paradise or in Hell as a repayment for what they did in this world. Here, we are talking about infinity—not about a hundred years, a hundred thousand years, millions or even billions of years. That is, even if there were hundreds of trillions of people destined to live for a trillion years, they still would be unable to determine the exact limit of infinity.

However, Allah has such a vast knowledge that everything we consider "infinite" is within His knowledge. From the moment that time was created until eternity, Allah determines every event, thought, and moment of time, as the Qur'an proclaims:

> We have created all things in due measure. Our command is only one word, like the blinking of an eye. We destroyed those of your kind in the past. But is there any rememberer there? Everything they did is in the Books. Everything is recorded, large or small. (Surat al-Qamar, 54:49-53)
>
> Then when He granted them a healthy, upright child, they associated what He had given them with Him. But Allah is far above what they associate with Him! (Surat al-A'raf, 7:190)
>
> He Who guides you in the darkness of land and sea and sends out the winds bringing advance news of His mercy. Is there another deity besides Allah? May Allah be exalted above what they associate with Him! (Surat an-Naml, 27:63)
>
> Allah created you, then provides for you, then will cause you to die, and then will bring you back to life. Can any of your partner-deities do any of that? Glory be to Him, and may He be exalted above anything they associate with Him! (Surat ar-Rum, 30:40)

AL-MUTAKABBIR
He Who Reveals His Greatness in All

He is Allah—there is no deity but Him. He is the King, the Most Pure, the Perfect Peace, the Trustworthy, the Safeguarder, the Almighty, the Compeller, **the Supremely Great**. Glory be to Allah above all they associate with Him. (Surat al-Hashr, 59:23)

Allah describes His greatness through the examples He gives in the Qur'an. For example, when Prophet Musa (as) requested **"My Lord, show me Yourself so that I may look at You!"** Allah replied: **"You will not see Me, but look at the mountain. If it remains firm in its place, then you will see Me."** The rest of the account is related, as follows:

... But when His Lord manifested Himself to the mountain, He crushed it flat and Musa fell unconscious to the ground. When he regained consciousness, he said: "Glory be to You!..." (Surat al-A'raf, 7:143)

When Prophet Ibrahim (as) said: **"My Lord, show me how You bring the dead to life,"** Allah replied: **"Take four birds and train them to yourself. Then put a part of them on each mountain and call to them; they will come rushing to you. Know that Allah is Almighty, All-Wise."** (Surat al-Baqara, 2:260) This way, Allah showed him a sign of His greatness.

Allah told Prophet Lut (as) to leave his city early in the morning with the believers and not to look back. That morning, He destroyed the unbelieving nation and rescued Prophet Lut (as). Allah made the fire coolness and peace for Prophet Ibrahim (as). By the hands of

Prophet 'Isa (as), He healed the blind and brought the dead to life. In the time of Prophet Musa (as), He parted the sea and drowned Pharaoh's army. This is how Allah manifests His greatness and part of His infinite power.

Allah openly reveals His greatness and power at every moment and in every incident. At dawn, He sends a hurricane toward those who greedily feel attached to this life of the world, or turns their cities upside down and makes them uninhabitable. This way, He strips them of their possessions and goods.

He submerges an entire city by pouring a heavy rain upon it, or ruins it by sending a great earthquake. The skies and the ground, the wind and the rain, all of which act under His surveillance, bring an unseen destruction to that city, and its people witness Allah's overwhelming power. No doubt, Allah is *al-Mutakabbir*. In the face of His power and strength, no one can become arrogant. He is the sole authority before Whom all will prostrate.

AL-MUSAWWIR
The Shaper; The Proportioner

O man! What has deluded you in respect of your Noble Lord? He Who created you and formed you and **proportioned you**. (Surah al-Infitar, 82:6-7)

A human being comes into being from the union of a sperm and an egg, which results in a single cell. This cell, as the Qur'an informs us, first looks like a lump of flesh. Then, Allah transforms it, makes it develop in the womb for a specified time, and then brings it forth as a human being. This new being is perfect in every way. As Allah proclaims:

Allah made Earth a stable home for you and the sky a dome, formed you, gave you the best of forms, and provided you with good and wholesome things. That is Allah, your Lord. Blessed be Allah, the Lord of all the worlds. (Surah Ghafir, 40:64)

As the Qur'an informs us, humanity was given the best form of all living beings on Earth and Allah displays countless signs of His creation both inside and outside the human body. Even the human body displays Allah's perfect artistry. Consider its symmetry: Its legs and arms, as well as the ratio of the body to the arms, legs, and head, are strikingly perfect. For instance, the length of the body is eight times the head's length. The length of the head is three times the length of the nose, and there is a distance of one eye between the two eyes. The ratio and length of our legs and arms are both aesthetic and fully functional.

In order to see this symmetry's perfect details, it is enough to gaze at the people around you. Indeed, these details were—and continue to be—typical of each person who has ever lived and who will live in the future, for this is how Allah creates. And, Allah's creation is flawless. Some of the verses regarding Allah's perfect creation are as follows:

> He created and molded. (Surat al-A'la, 87:2)
>
> He created the heavens and Earth with truth and formed you, giving you the best of forms. And He is your final destination. (Surat at-Taghabun, 64:3)
>
> He forms you in the womb however He wills. There is no deity but Him, the Almighty, the All-Wise. (Surah Al 'Imran, 3:6)
>
> He is Allah—the Creator, the Maker, the Giver of Form. To Him belong the Most Beautiful Names. Everything in the heavens and Earth glorifies Him. He is the Almighty, the All-Wise. (Surat al-Hashr, 59:24)

AL-MUSTI'AN
One Who Is Called upon for Help

Say: "Lord, judge with truth! Our Lord is the All-Merciful, the One Whose help is sought in the face of what you describe." (Surat al-Anbiya', 21:112)

People need to feel Allah's existence and power both in times of difficulty and of ease. In other words, during every moment of their lives, all people are in need of prayer, for unless Allah wills, they cannot attain anything. Given that we are created with many inherent weaknesses, people can only live by means of Allah's mercy and favor.

On the other hand, Allah is the sole Deity in Whom one can take refuge. People are in need of Him, and therefore seek help and guidance only from Him. Without His permission, no one can help himself or someone else. Allah has the strength to make anything at any time He wills. When He decides on something, He just says to it "Be!" and it is.

He allocates provisions among His servants, pours down rain from the heavens, and grants blessings. He heals people when they are sick, makes them laugh or shed tears, exalts whoever He wills, and directs all affairs from heaven to Earth. No one can protect themselves if our Lord withholds His blessings or sends a disaster, and no one can deflect a blessing if He wills to bestow it. Thus, the universe and all of its inhabitants, whether living or non-living, takes refuge in Him and asks for help only from Him. The Qur'an reveals these facts, as follows:

Do they make things into partner-deities who cannot create

anything and are themselves created; who are not capable of helping them and cannot even help themselves? If you call them to guidance, they will not follow you. It makes no difference if you call them or stay silent. Those you call on besides Allah are servants, just like yourselves. Call on them and let them respond to you, if you are telling the truth. Do they have legs with which they can walk? Do they have hands with which they can grasp? Do they have eyes with which they can see? Do they have ears with which they can hear? Say: "Call on your partner-deities, try all your wiles against me, and grant me no reprieve. My Protector is Allah, Who sent down the Book. He takes care of the believers." Those you call on besides Him are not capable of helping you. They cannot even help themselves. If you call them to guidance, they do not hear. You see them looking at you, yet they do not see. (Surat al-A'raf, 7:191-98)

AL-MUTAHHIR
The Cleanser; He Who Cleanses from Idolatry and Spiritual Evil

And when He overcame you with sleep, making you feel secure, and sent down water from heaven **to purify you and remove the taint of Satan from you**, and to fortify your hearts and make your feet firm. (Surat al-Anfal, 8:11)

Human beings make mistakes throughout their lives. No doubt, believers make every effort to avoid such mistakes and strive not to commit them by living according to Allah's religion. This fact is related in the Qur'an, as follows:

If Allah were to take mankind to task for what they have earned, He would not leave a single creature crawling on it; but He defers them until a specified time. Then, when their time comes, Allah sees His servants! (Surah Fatir, 35:45)

In compliance with this divine command, sincere believers are not expected to be infallible or sinless; rather, they are expected to seek Allah's pleasure, abide by the limits that He has established for them, turn to Allah in repentance, and take refuge in His mercy. As the Qur'an informs, Allah will purify them, for Allah "desires to remove all impurity from His servants." This is related in the following verse:

... Allah desires to remove all impurity from you, O People of the House, and to purify you completely. (Surat al-Ahzab, 33:33)

Although a person may have committed great sins, rebelled against Allah, and lived by principles that are utterly contrary to

Allah and His religion, Allah is so compassionate that He may purify those of His servants who sincerely repent. Furthermore, Allah informs us that He may even purify and forgive unbelievers and hypocrites who have fought Him and His religion if they ever turn to Him with a sincere heart. One verse reads:

The hypocrites are in the lowest level of the Fire. You will not find anyone to help them. Except those who repent, put things right, hold fast to Allah, and dedicate their religion to Allah alone; they are with the believers. Allah will give the believers an immense reward. (Surat an-Nisa', 4:145-46)

These words are manifestations of Allah's infinite mercy toward His servants. Clearly, only He can purify His servants from idolatry, evil, and spiritual uncleanliness. Allah is the most compassionate of the Compassionate.

AL-MUYASSIR
He Who Makes His Servant's Path Easier in Goodness and Wickedness; He Who Places No Unbearable Burden on Anyone

Allah desires ease for you; He does not desire difficulty for you. You should complete the number of days and proclaim Allah's greatness for the guidance He has given you, so that hopefully you will be thankful. (Surat al-Baqara, 2:185)

Allah always directs us toward ease. At the base of Islam, the religion with which He is pleased, always lies this ease. The Qur'an reveals this profound truth, as follows:

Strive for Allah with the effort due to Him. He has selected you and has not placed any constraint upon you in religion—the religion of your forefather Ibrahim... (Surat al-Hajj, 22:78)

Allah has made the Qur'an easy for those who are willing to take heed, and its commands make human life easy. For instance, He does not hold the blind, the lame, or the sick responsible, and shows ways that lessen His servants' burden during times of hardship and travel. He also states that He will forgive people, whatever their sins may be, provided that they repent sincerely. One verse reads:

We have made the Qur'an easy to remember. But is there any rememberer there? (Surat al-Qamar, 54:17)

Meanwhile, Allah calls attention to the fact that believers can easily attain all forms of success:

We will ease you to the Easy Way. (Surat al-A'la, 87:8)

Every ease that we feel or see is from Allah, for they all come from His glory. He is the Most Compassionate of the compassionate, and He does not desire difficulty for His servants:

Allah desires to make things lighter for you. Man was created weak. (Surat an-Nisa', 4:28)

Allah knows what we can and cannot do, and thus does not desire any difficulty for us. This is also related in **"Allah desires ease for you; He does not desire difficulty for you"** (Surat al-Baqara, 2:185). Even under the severest conditions, He makes our tasks easy and shows us a way out. Allah reminds His servants of this blessings in the following verses:

Did We not expand your breast for you and remove your load from you, which weighed down your back? Did We not raise your renown high? For truly with hardship comes ease; truly with hardship comes ease. (Surat al-Inshirah, 94:1-6)

Allah makes the ways of attaining His good pleasure and mercy easy for believers. On the other hand, He informs us that He will pave the way to difficulty for unbelievers:

But as for him who is stingy, self-satisfied, and denies the Good, We will pave his way to difficulty. (Surat al-Layl, 92:8-10)

AL-MUZAKKEE
He Who Purifies His Servants (of all faults, shame, and spiritual impurity)

Do you not see those who claim to be purified? No, **Allah purifies whoever He wills**. They will not be wronged by so much as the smallest speck. (Surat an-Nisa', 4:49)

Infallibility and perfection are qualities unique to Allah. We may forget, become heedless, and make mistakes, but Allah does not. Such traits indicate our weakness and need of Allah in every situation. Given this, believers feel regret once they recognize their mistakes, repent, and are careful not to repeat them. Just considering themselves sinless and faultless is a great sin in itself. One verse reads:

> **To whoever avoids the major sins and indecencies—except for minor lapses, truly your Lord is vast in forgiveness. He has the most knowledge of you when He first produced you from dust and when you were embryos in your mothers' wombs. So do not claim purity for yourselves. He knows best those who guard against evil. (Surat an-Najm, 53:32)**

Sincere believers are conscious of their mistakes and weaknesses. For this reason, they repent continuously and pray for Allah's mercy and good pleasure. In return, Allah covers their mistakes, forgives their sins, purifies them, and enables them to attain a superior position.

AL-MUZAYYIN
The Adorner

Know that the Messenger of Allah is among you. If he were to obey you in many things, you would suffer for it. However, Allah has given you the love of faith and **has made it pleasing to your hearts,** and has made disbelief, deviance, and disobedience hateful to you. People such as these are rightly guided. (Surat al-Hujurat, 49:7)

Loving faith, deriving pleasure from material and spiritual tastes, as well as hating disbelief and seeing it as evil, seem to be natural inclinations. However, they actually are blessings attained by Allah's favor. Allah relates this metaphysical truth in the verse quoted above.

In order to show the value of this great blessing and gift to believers, Allah creates the opposite situation for unbelievers. Failing to see the beauties engendered by faith, unbelievers derive pleasure from the gloomy and troublesome system of those who are far from religion. All of the evil and indecency found in the systems of unbelief have been made to seem good to them. This secret is divulged in the Qur'an, as follows:

Is someone on a clear path from his Lord like those whose bad actions have been made to seem good to them and who follow their own desires? (Surah Muhammad, 47:14)

Believers, who know Allah, notice His compassion for them, recognize that they exist only by His will, and that everything they like and take pleasure in come from Him. They attain the superiority of Allah's love and faith. Believers do not need to please anyone other than Allah, and so they ask for no other being's help. Indeed, people find peace only in the remembrance of Allah. They consider doing good deeds in order to earn Allah's good pleasure, living by His religion's code of moral excellence, observing His commands and prohibitions, being concerned about their fellow Muslims, and striving for the Hereafter as sources of joy and happiness.

AL-MUDHHILL
The Humiliator

You may travel about in the land for four months and know that you cannot thwart Allah, and that **Allah will humiliate the unbelievers.** (Surat at-Tawba, 9:2)

Humiliation is one of the punishments that Allah sends to unbelievers in this world. For unbelievers who are devoted to ostentation and seeking others' approval, humiliation is a very severe punishment. In the Qur'an, Allah describes this punishment, as follows:

Those before them also denied the truth, and the punishment came upon them from where they did not expect. So Allah made them taste disgrace in the life of the world, and the punishment of the Hereafter is far worse, if they only knew. (Surat az-Zumar, 39:25-26)

Allah manifests this attribute through believers and especially through those of His Messengers. The following verses call attention to this fact, as follows:

... Allah will punish them at your hands, disgrace them, help you against them, and heal the hearts of those who believe. He will remove the rage from their hearts. Allah turns to anyone He wills. Allah is All-Knowing, All-Wise. (Surat at-Tawba, 9:14-15)

The message Prophet Sulayman (as) sent to the unbelievers was as follows:

"Return to them. We will come to them with troops they cannot face, and will expel them from it, abased and humil-

iated." (Surat an-Naml, 27:37)

On the other hand, in many verses Allah gives the news of a degrading punishment awaiting unbelievers in the Hereafter, one that they deserve because of their arrogance and pride in this world. As stated earlier, one of the unbelievers' major goals is to gain other people's appreciation, and so they praise themselves rather than glorify Allah. Thus, Allah makes humiliation the essence of their punishment in Hell, for their humiliation in front of other people will cause them to experience the greatest anguish. One verse reads:

On the Day when those who were unbelievers are exposed to the Fire: "You dissipated the good things you had in your worldly life, and enjoyed yourself in it. So today you are being repaid with the punishment of humiliation for being arrogant in the land, without any right, and for being deviators." (Surat al-Ahqaf, 46:20)

The humiliation and abasement experienced in Hell is unprecedented and of various kinds. This humiliation will even manifest itself upon their bodies. For example, dust and debasement will darken their faces, as the following verses reveal:

Some faces on that Day will be downcast. (Surat al-Ghashiya, 88:2)

But as for those who have earned bad actions—a bad action will be repaid with one like it. Debasement will darken them. They will have no one to protect them from Allah. It is as if their faces were covered by dark patches of night. Those are the Companions of the Fire, remaining in it timelessly, forever. (Surah Yunus, 10:27)

While manifesting His attribute of *al-Mudhhill* upon unbelievers, Allah manifests His names of *ar-Rahman* and *ar-Rahman ar-Raheem* upon believers. By granting His Paradise and mercy, our

Lord purifies them of all forms of evil. Contrary to the unbelievers' humiliation, Allah will grant His sincere servants His good pleasure, Paradise, and blessings.

AL-MUGHNEE
The Enricher

That it is **He Who enriches** and Who satisfies. (Surat an-Najm, 53:48)

Allah, the true Owner of all wealth, tests some people with wealth and others with poverty. In His capacity of *al-Warith* (the Inheritor), Allah is the sole inheritor of everything. When people die, they leave behind all of their possessions. As for those who take pride in their possessions and wealth and thus fail to remember Allah, the Qur'an relates the following:

Do they imagine that, in the wealth and children We extend to them, We are hastening to them with good things? No indeed, but they have no awareness! (Surat al-Mu'minun, 23:55-56)

Allah may reward whomever He wills with great wealth. The Qur'an calls attention to the great wealth granted to such Messengers as Prophet Ibrahim (as), Prophet Muhammad (saas), Prophet Dawud (as), and Prophet Yusuf (as). Prophet Sulayman (as), on the other hand, asked for unprecedented wealth, and Allah answered his prayer.

One point deserves special mention here: Allah's Messengers used their wealth to attain His good pleasure by doing good deeds. However, unbelievers take pride in their wealth and forget its real owner.

The Qur'an gives a detailed account of the wealth that a few people, who deserve to earn Allah's good pleasure and thereby attain Paradise, will enjoy in the Hereafter. This glory is depicted in the following verses:

> So Allah has safeguarded them from the evil of that Day, has made them meet with radiance and pure joy, and will reward them for their steadfastness with a garden and with silk. Reclining in it on couches, they will experience neither burning sun nor bitter cold. Its shading branches will droop down over them, its ripe fruit hanging ready to be picked. Vessels of silver and goblets of pure crystal will be passed round among them, crystalline silver—they have measured them very exactly. They will be given a cup to drink mixed with the warmth of ginger. In it is a flowing spring called Salsabil. Ageless youths will circulate among them, serving them. Seeing them, you would think them scattered pearls. Seeing them, you see delight and a great kingdom. They will wear green garments of fine silk and rich brocade. They will be adorned with silver bracelets. And their Lord will give them a pure draught to drink. "This is your reward. Your striving is fully acknowledged." (Surat al-Insan, 76:11-22)

AN-NASIR
The Helper; The Supporter

We supported them, and so they were the victors. (Surat as-Saffat, 37:116)

Allah is our sole helper and guardian. In all difficulties and situations, believers ask for His help and He accepts their call. In order to establish justice, acquire property and recover from an illness so that they could pursue Allah's good pleasure, the Prophets turned to Allah alone. In return, He answered their sincere calls and guided them at all times. Allah promises the following in His book:

> **Our Word was given before to Our servants, the Messengers, that they would certainly be helped.** (Surat as-Saffat, 37:171-72)
>
> **In this way, We have assigned to every Prophet an enemy from among the evildoers. But your Lord is a sufficient guide and helper.** (Surat al-Furqan, 25:31)

In "... **it is Our duty to help the believers**" (Surat ar-Rum, 30:47), Allah states that He will help His believing servants. However, among the most important prerequisites for earning Allah's good pleasure is to help His religion, observe His limits meticulously, and strive for this cause. In return, He always helps them. As Allah promises, victory belongs only to those who believe in our Lord and struggle to attain His good pleasure and consent. One verse reads:

> **Allah has promised those of you who believe and do right actions that He will make them successors in the land, just as He made those before them successors; will firmly estab-**

lish for them their religion, with which He is pleased; and will give them, in place of their fear, security. "They worship Me, not associating anything with Me." Any who do not believe after that, such people are deviators. **(Surat an-Nur, 24:55)**

Allah does not leave believers alone and helpless in this world. Rather, He promises to help them both in this world and beyond. And, as He states, He keeps His promises:

We will certainly help Our Messengers and those who believe both in the life of the world and on the Day the witnesses appear. (Surah Ghafir, 40:51)

AN-NUR
The Light

Allah is the Light of the heavens and Earth. The metaphor of His Light is that of a niche in which is a lamp, the lamp inside a glass, the glass like a brilliant star, lit from a blessed tree, an olive, neither of the east nor of the west, its oil all but giving off light even if no fire touches it. **Light upon Light.** Allah guides to His Light whoever He wills, makes metaphors for mankind, and has knowledge of all things. In houses that Allah has permitted to be built and in which His name is remembered, there are men who proclaim His glory morning and evening. (Surat an-Nur, 24:35-36)

Allah, the Light of the heavens and Earth, manifests this attribute upon people. As a blessing, He illuminates His servants who believe in Him, recognize and appreciate His greatness, turn to Islam (the only just religion), and live by its morality:

Is he whose breast is opened to Islam, and who is therefore illuminated by his Lord...? Woe to those whose hearts are hardened against the remembrance of Allah! Such people are clearly misguided. (Surat az-Zumar, 39:22)

For the unbelievers, however, there is not a single source of "illumination." Moreover, they cannot find a way out of the darkness in which they exist. Allah describes this darkness in the following terms:

Or they are like the darkness of a fathomless sea that is covered by waves above, which are waves above which are clouds, layers of darkness, one upon the other. If he puts

out his hand, he can scarcely see it. Those to whom Allah gives no light, they have no light. (Surat an-Nur, 24:40)

While Allah leaves unbelievers in this darkness, He guides His faithful servants to the light. The following verse reveals that these two groups are mirror opposites and believers are absolutely superior, for:

Is someone who was dead and whom We brought to life, supplying him with a light by which to walk among people, the same as someone who is in utter darkness, unable to emerge from it? That is how what they were doing is made to seem attractive to the unbelievers. (Surat al-An'am, 6:122)

Allah sends down warnings to believers in order to guide them to the light. His Messengers and the just Books that they bring are all sources of "light." Those who comply with the divine message attain the true path and are illuminated. The Qur'an proclaims:

O Prophet! We have sent you as a witness, a bringer of good news, a warner, a caller to Allah by His permission, and a light-giving lamp. (Surat al-Ahzab, 33:45-46)

He sends down Clear Signs to His servant to bring you out of the darkness to the light. Allah is All-Gentle with you, Most Merciful. (Surat al-Hadid, 57:9)

O People of the Book! Our Messenger has come to you, making clear to you much of the Book that you have kept concealed, and passing over a lot. A Light has come to you from Allah, and a Clear Book. By it, Allah guides those who follow what pleases Him to the ways of peace. He will bring them from the darkness to the light by His permission, and guide them to a straight path. (Surat al-Ma'ida, 5:15-16)

Allah's true servants will live happily until they die, and will be recognized by their light. Unbelievers, on the other hand, will remain in infinite darkness in the Hereafter as well, and will ask believers for some of their light. As the Qur'an states:

> On the Day you see the men and women of the believers, with their light streaming out in front of them, and to their right: "Good news for you today of gardens with rivers flowing under them, remaining in them timelessly, forever. That is the Great Victory." That Day, the men and women of the hypocrites will say to those who believe: "Wait for us so that we can borrow some of your light." They will be told: "Go back and look for light!" And a wall will be erected between them with a gate in it, on the inside of which there will be mercy but before whose exterior lies punishment. (Surat al-Hadid, 57:12-13)

> Allah is the Protector of those who believe. He brings them out of the darkness and into the light. But those who are unbelievers have false deities as protectors. They take them from the light into the darkness. Those are the Companions of the Fire, remaining in it timelessly, forever. (Surat al-Baqara, 2:257)

> He calls down blessing upon you, as do His angels, to bring you out of the darkness and into the light. He is Most Merciful to the believers. (Surat al-Ahzab, 33:43)

> And Earth will shine with the Pure Light of its Lord, the Book will be put in place, the Prophets and witnesses will be brought, and it will be decided between them with the truth. They will not be wronged. (Surat az-Zumar, 39:69)

> Those who believe in Allah and His Messengers—such people are the truly sincere—and the martyrs who are with their Lord will receive their wages and their light. But those

who are unbelievers and deny Our Signs will be Companions of the Blazing Fire. (Surat al-Hadid, 57:19)

O You who believe! Have fear [and awareness] of Allah and faith in His Messenger. He will give you a double portion of His mercy, grant you a Light by which to walk, and forgive you. Allah is Ever-Forgiving, Most Merciful. (Surat al-Hadid, 57:28)

Prophet Muhammad (saas) advises believers to say the following in their prayers:

"Allahumma: Put light in my heart, light in my tongue, light in my sight, light in my hearing, light on my right, light on my left, light above me, light beneath me, light in front of me, and light behind me. Put light in my soul, and give me great light." (Sahih Bukhari and Sahih Muslim)

RABB AL-'ALIMEEN
Lord of All the Worlds

All praise belongs to Allah, the Lord of the heavens and the Lord of Earth, **Lord of all the worlds.** All greatness belongs to Him in the heavens and Earth. He is the Almighty, the All-Wise. (Surat al-Jathiya, 45:36-37)

Our universe contains many other worlds of which humanity is utterly ignorant. For example, each plant and animal species contains numerous subspecies. Even such inanimate objects as winds and clouds have many different types. Just like people, all things might be said to live in universes of their own.

This aside, Allah created the invisible world of atoms, cells with glorious systems that form our body, and hundreds of other microscopic living beings. He is the Lord of a coral colony in the depths of the ocean, just as He controls the infinite number of micro-universes of invisible organisms, to the macro-universes of celestial bodies. He feeds all of their inhabitants and causes them to survive. The Qur'an, which proclaims that Allah is the Lord of all the worlds, states:

Allah made Earth a stable home for you and the sky a dome; formed you, giving you the best of forms; and provided you with good and wholesome things. That is Allah, your Lord. Blessed be Allah, the Lord of all the worlds. He is the Living—there is no deity but Him—so call on Him, making your religion sincerely His. Praise be to Allah, the Lord of all the worlds. (Surah Ghafir, 40:64-65)

People who ponder over the oceans and its inhabitants, their lives and food, the symbiosis they experience, the delicate balance, their reproduction and continued existence, appreciate Allah's infinite power.

Allah, the Lord of the universes as well as of the jinn and angels that exist in an utterly different time and space, created all of these beings and made them submit to Him. These universes, all works of His artistry and infinite power, are far beyond our wisdom and imagination. Faced with this greatness, we are obliged to turn to Allah, as Prophet Ibrahim (as) did. When Allah called him to submit, he said: "**... I am a Muslim who has submitted to the Lord of all the worlds.**" (Surat al-Baqara, 2:131)

After that, we should strive to devote our lives to earning His good pleasure, for:

Say: "My prayer and my rites, my living and my dying, are for Allah alone, the Lord of all the worlds." (Surat al-An'am, 6:162)

So the last remnant of the people who did wrong was cut off. Praise belongs to Allah, the Lord of all the worlds! (Surat al-An'am, 6:45)

Your Lord is Allah, Who created the heavens and Earth in six days and then settled Himself firmly on the Throne. He covers the day with the night, each pursuing the other urgently; and the Sun and the Moon and stars are subservient to His command. Both creation and command belong to Him. Blessed be Allah, the Lord of all the worlds. (Surat al-A'raf, 7:54)

AR-RAFI'
The Exalter; The Raiser

Mention Idris in the Book. He was a true man and a Prophet. **We raised him up to a high place.** (Surah Maryam, 19:56-57)

People who are ignorant of religion lead a life that is far from Allah. Therefore, they neither observe His commands and prohibitions nor appreciate the countless blessings He grants out of His favor. Unable to think or exercise spiritual intelligence, they cannot appreciate Allah's glory.

Throughout history, Allah has sent Messengers to all societies to convey His commands, prohibitions, and recommendations. In this way, He calls upon people who are far from religion to abandon their ignorance and lack of knowledge and then grants them another opportunity to follow the straight path. These Messengers were members of the nations to which they were sent, and were known for their moral excellence, wisdom, and superior conscience. As the Qur'an states many times, Messengers are people chosen by Allah to warn their people. They are distinguished from their fellows by being the first to notice Allah's existence and greatness, and the nearness of the Hereafter. These features reveal their superiority.

After being granted prophethood, the Messengers called their people to the right path and warned them of the punishment of Hell. The difficulties that they faced, the hardships that the insolent unbelievers placed in their paths, and even the attempts on their lives never diverted them from the right path. On the contrary, such events deepened their faith. At times, Messengers met people who said: "We are Muslims submitted to our Lord," but then suddenly deserted them when they encountered some difficulty. But they persevered, for these chosen servants of Allah were **"on a sure footing with the Lord"** (Surah Yunus, 10:2) and wholly submitted to Him.

In return for their sincerity and trust, Allah made them distinguished both in this world and in the Hereafter. The related verses read:

> This is the argument We gave to Ibrahim against his people. We raise in rank anyone We will. Your Lord is All-Wise, All-Knowing. We gave him Ishaq and Ya'qub, each of whom We guided. And before him We had guided Nuh. And among his descendants were Dawud and Sulayman, and Ayyub, Yusuf, Musa, and Harun. That is how We recompense the good-doers. And Zakariyya, Yahya, 'Isa, and Ilyas. All of them were among the righteous. And Isma'il, al-Yasa', Yunus, and Lut. All of them We favored over all beings. (Surat al-An'am, 6:83-85)

AR-RAHMAN AR-RAHEEM
The Most Gracious, the Most Merciful

He is Allah—there is no deity but Him. He is the Knower of the Unseen and the Visible. He is the All-Merciful, **the Most Merciful**. (Surat al-Hashr, 59:22)

Allah, the Most Gracious, manifests His infinite mercy and favor upon whatever He wills. We can survive only through this influx of visible and invisible blessings, all of which are submissive to Allah.

Allah encompasses His creation every day through His blessings. He causes millions of seeds to sprout, covers the earth's core with a temperature of 4,500° Celsius (8,132° Fahrenheit) with this fertile earth, pours down tons of clear water upon Earth's surface, simultaneously feeds countless living beings all over the world, creates the oxygen that circulates in our lungs, and sends countless other blessings that give life.

Allah creates every one of the 100 trillion cells that make up the human body and then teaches every one of them their individual tasks; places DNA, which comprises information that would fill a million pages, in the cell; makes this system operate through protein, fat, and water molecules that He puts in a cube far smaller than 1 millimeter (0.03 inch); and gives each person a soul and keeps them alive until He wills otherwise.

From their birth to their death, each person receives and lives with Allah's blessings. Some see these blessings, grasp the purpose of their existence, and thereby devote themselves to Allah. Others do not, and so remain ungrateful and reject serving Him. Despite this, however, Allah manifests His graciousness upon all people, regardless of whether they are unbelievers, hypocrites, or polytheists. For example, He provides all people with air to breathe, water to drink, houses to live in, children, health, beauty, and many other blessings. This manifests His name "the Most Gracious."

Prophet Muhammad (saas) says in a hadith:

"Allah is more merciful to His servants than a mother is to her child." (Sahih Bukhari and Sahih Muslim)

In this life, Allah also grants blessings so that people may turn to religion, think, use their intellect, and thank Him. Those who turn away have only a short time, as short as the blink of an eye, to take advantage of these blessings. In the Hereafter, however, all blessings belong to believers who strove to draw near to Allah and earn His good pleasure while in this arena of testing. They give thanks to our Lord, for Allah is the Most Gracious and gives the good news of Paradise only to His faithful servants.

Gardens of Eden, which the All-Merciful has promised to His servants in the Unseen. His promise is always kept. (Surah Maryam, 19:61)

The All-Compassionate, the Most Merciful. (Surat al-Fatiha, 1:2)

Say: "Call upon Allah or call on the All-Merciful; whichever you call upon, the Most Beautiful Names are His." Do not be too loud in your prayer or too quiet in it, but try to find a way between the two. (Surat al-Isra', 17:110)

On that day they will follow the summoner, who has no crookedness in him at all. Voices will be humbled before the All-Merciful, and nothing but a whisper will be heard. (Surah Ta Ha, 20:108)

Say: "Lord, judge with truth! Our Lord is the All-Merciful, the One Whose help is sought in the face of what you describe." (Surat al-Anbiya', 21:112)

On the Day when the Spirit and the angels stand in ranks, no one will speak, except for him who is authorized by the All-Merciful and says what is right. (Surat an-Naba, 78:38)

AR-RAQEEB
The Watchful

O mankind! Have fear [and awareness] of your Lord, Who created you from a single self, created its mate from it, and then disseminated many men and women from the two of them. Heed Allah, in Whose name you make demands on one another and also in respect of your families. **Allah watches over you continually.** (Surat an-Nisa', 4:1)

Allah protects and watches all beings; controls, watches, witnesses, and supervises everything from the stars and solar systems to atmospheric events and to the societies and plants covering this planet, and from the human body's complex and complicated systems to the micro- and macro-universes that are invisible to the naked eye.

People may think that they are not responsible to anyone, and thus may live without a purpose. But regardless of what they are doing, Allah sees them, for nothing can be hidden from His Sight. Allah repays anything done with justice, for He has comprehensive knowledge. Many people think that Allah created the universe and then left it to its own devices. Yet this is only a delusion and an assumption.

Allah knows every invisible cell down to its minute details. While functioning in perfect harmony with the trillions of other cells in the body, one day a cell can no longer control its replication and thus causes cancer. We have no control over such developments, but Allah knows all of this and controls every phase. Just as a person cannot take a step without Allah's will, that cell cannot function without His will. Given that He is the Creator, Allah knows everything and is the sole source of all knowledge. No being can do anything without Him knowing it. One verse reads:

... Allah is watchful over all things. (Surat al-Ahzab, 33:52)

AR-RA'UF
The Gentle

In this way, We have made you a middlemost community so that you may act as witnesses against mankind, and the Messenger [may act] as a witness against you. We only appointed the direction you used to face in order to distinguish those who follow the Messenger from those who turn back on their heels. Though in truth it is a very hard thing—except for those Allah has guided. Allah would never let your faith go to waste. **Allah is All-Gentle,** Most Merciful to mankind. (Surat al-Baqara, 2:143)

All beings owe their existence to Allah's superior creation and the ensuing complex structures. This is one sign of our Lord's mercy and compassion, since no living being is responsible for its own survival but must submit to Allah's Will. Allah has already given every being whatever it needs. For instance, all living beings have various means of self-defense, such as a startling appearance, poisonous or flammable gasses, high levels of alertness and the ability to outrun their enemies, strong shields, camouflage, or the ability to play dead.

Living beings did not acquire these features coincidentally or by themselves. Allah, Who creates everything flawlessly and with great knowledge, reveals His compassion by endowing them with attributes that enable them to lead their lives comfortably.

Aside from these attributes, one notices that whatever has been created to serve humanity is also superior. Indeed, people who ponder over the material and spiritual attributes they enjoy readily notice that they live in a world that was created especially for them. The fact that our survival is assured is one of the greatest signs of Allah's mercy. However, apart from our five senses, Allah has enabled us to think, an ability that makes us superior to all other living beings. Allah relates His attribute of *ar-Rauf* in the verses below, as follows:

> On the Day that each self finds the good it did and the evil it did present in front of it, it will wish that there were an age between it and them. Allah advises you to beware of Him. Allah is Ever-Gentle with His servants. (Surah Al 'Imran, 3:30)

> Do you not see that Allah has made everything on Earth subservient to you, and the ships running upon the sea by His command? He holds back the heaven, preventing it from falling to the ground—except by His permission. Allah is All-Compassionate to mankind, Most Merciful. (Surat al-Hajj, 22:65)

> He sends down Clear Signs to His servant to bring you out of the darkness and into to the light. Allah is All-Gentle with you, Most Merciful. (Surat al-Hadid, 57:9)

AR-RAZZAQ
The All-Provider

Truly, **Allah is the Provider,** the Possessor of Strength, the Sure. (Surat adh-Dhariyat, 51:58)

Imagine that you open your eyes in a world without mountains or oceans; with black, very dry and barren land; without animals or food for human beings, except for grass; and with infertile soil and water located hundreds of kilometers away. In order to survive, you would eat only that bitter grass and walk hundreds of kilometers to drink water. And, after a life of hardship, you would die. Interestingly, you would never ask: "Why can't we grow juicy, delicious fruits, vegetables, and various other crops in this land?" because you would not even be aware that the land could yield such crops.

Allah, Who is very compassionate and merciful toward His servants, places people on fertile lands that yield countless blessings. Indeed, even without tilling them, lands yield green crops and clusters of flowers. Yellow, red, green, and orange fruits and vegetables come out of the soil, and the blue oceans abound with tasty fish. These aside, Allah places the meat of most animals and birds at our service, and gives them pure milk and honey. All of these are all blessings from Allah.

As Allah informs us in **"Who is there who could provide for you if He withholds His provision? Yet still they obstinately persist in insolence and evasion"** (Surat al-Mulk, 67:21), if He wills, lands do not yield crops, rain does not fall, and soil turns barren. But since Allah is Most Gracious, Most Merciful, it is impossible to number His blessings. He commands in the Qur'an, as follows:

> O mankind! Remember Allah's blessing to you. Is there any creator other than Allah providing for you from heaven and earth? There is no deity but Him. So how have you been deluded? (Surah Fatir, 35:3)

These blessings, which are granted in this world, have perfect counterparts in the Hereafter, as the Qur'an tells us:

> No self knows the delight that is hidden away for it in recompense for what it used to do. (Surat as-Sajda, 32:17)

The inhabitants of Hell, on the other hand, will have nothing to eat and drink but the tree of *az-Zaqqum*, boiling water, and bitter thorny bush for all eternity.

> Say: "Who provides for you out of heaven and earth? Who controls hearing and sight? Who brings forth the living from the dead and the dead from the living? Who directs the whole affair?" They will say: "Allah." Say: "So will you not guard against evil?" (Surah Yunus, 10:31)

> So that Allah can reward them for the best of what they did and give them more from His unbounded favor. Allah provides for anyone He wills without reckoning. (Surat an-Nur, 24:38)

AS-SAMAD
The Everlasting Refuge and Sustainer

Allah, the Everlasting Sustainer of all. (Surat al-Ikhlas, 112:2)

In the entire universe, all power belongs to Allah, the only One Who can remove a person's troubles and difficulties, and meet his needs. Sometimes people forget our Lord and take other guardians for themselves, who they believe can provide them with power, honor, and help. But this is a delusion, for there is no other deity other than Allah. Unless He wills otherwise, no one can help or harm anyone else. This fact is related in the Qur'an, as follows:

> Do those who take the hypocrites as protectors, rather than the believers, hope to find power and strength with them? Power and strength belong entirely to Allah. (Surat an-Nisa', 4:139)

Our only refuge from distress is Allah, the Lord of power and honor, for He answers all of His servants' prayers and eases, or fully removes, what is causing them hardship. Allah describes this, as follows:

> He Who responds to the oppressed when they call upon Him and removes their distress, and has appointed you as inheritors of the land. Is there another deity besides Allah? How little you pay heed! (Surat an-Naml, 27:62)

This verse states that some people fail to recognize or forget Allah's compassion and mercy and become ungrateful. However, as Allah states in **"Say: 'Allah rescues you from it, and from every plight'..."** (Surat al-An'am, 6:64), only He saves us from every distress. In return, He expects us to notice this answer, ponder over its importance, submit to Him, and become His grateful servant.

The Prophet (saas) advises believers to take refuge only in Allah:

"When you ask, ask from Allah; when you seek help, seek it of Allah." (Hadith at-Tirmidhi)

AS-SADIQ
The True; The Keeper of His Word

That is Allah's promise. **Allah does not break His promise.** But most people do not know it. (Surat ar-Rum, 30:6)

Allah created humanity and sent Messengers to enjoin good and forbid evil. He also sent Books to guide humanity to the straight path. The Qur'an, the last of these just Books, guides us from the darkness to the light, to the right path.

In the Qur'an, Allah makes promises to both believers and unbelievers. Unless He wills otherwise, unbelievers are promised a stressful life in this world and an eternal punishment in Hell. But because they have no faith in this promise, they assume that they will never be punished. Allah addresses these deluded people in the following terms:

They ask you to hasten the punishment. Allah will not break His promise... (Surat al-Hajj, 22:47)

Meanwhile, Allah promises believers a blissful life both in this world and in the next, as the following verses state:

Allah has promised those of you who believe and do right actions that He will make them successors in the land, just as He made those before them successors; will firmly establish for them their religion, with which He is pleased; and give them, in place of their fear, security. "They worship Me, not associating anything with Me." Any who do not believe after that, such people are deviators. (Surat an-Nur, 24:55)

But as for those who believe and do right actions, We will

admit them into gardens with rivers flowing under them, remaining in them timelessly, for ever and ever. Allah's promise is true. Whose speech could be truer than Allah's? (Surat an-Nisa', 4:122)

The Words of your Lord are perfect in truthfulness and justice. No one can change His Words. He is the All-Hearing, the All-Knowing. (Surat al-An'am, 6:115)

Say: "Allah speaks the truth, so follow the religion of Ibrahim, a man of pure natural belief. He was not one of the idolaters." (Surah Al 'Imran, 3:95)

AS-SA'IQ
The Driver; He Who Drives to Hell

But **We will drive the evildoers to Hell**, like cattle to a watering hole. (Surah Maryam, 19:86)

Humanity was created to serve Allah and has been placed here to be tested. Allah meets all of our needs and has granted us various blessings. Despite this, however, some people forget the purpose of their existence, become ungrateful, and rebel against Allah. Such rebellion has to be punished, for Allah is infinitely just. In the Qur'an, He reveals the end of those who grow arrogant, as follows:

As was the case with the people of Pharaoh and those before them. They denied Our Signs, so Allah seized them for their wrong actions. Allah is fierce in retribution. Say to those who are unbelievers: "You will be overwhelmed and crowded into Hell. What an evil resting-place!" (Surah Al 'Imran, 3:11-12)

Although granted countless opportunities and given many warnings to turn to the straight path, they insisted upon turning away and becoming arrogant. Thus, on the Day of Judgment,

...You will see the wrongdoers saying, when they see the punishment: "Is there no way back?" You will see them as they are exposed to it, abject in their abasement, glancing around them furtively. Those who believe will say: "Truly the losers are those who lose themselves and their families on the Day of Rising." The wrongdoers are in an everlasting punishment. (Surah ash-Shura, 42:44-45)

This situation manifests Allah's infinite justice. In one verse,

Allah relates that every person will receive whatever he or she deserves, as follows:

Allah does not wrong anyone by so much as the smallest speck. And if there is a good deed, Allah will multiply it and pay out an immense reward direct from Him. (Surat an-Nisa', 4:40)

As a requisite of this superior justice, Allah will host believers in infinite gardens abounding in unprecedented blessings. Allah gives this good news to believers who devote their lives to our Lord:

Give the good news to those who believe and do right actions that they will have gardens with rivers flowing under them. When they are given fruit as provision, they will say: "This is what we were given before." But they were only given a simulation of it. They will have spouses of perfect purity and will remain there timelessly, forever. (Surat al-Baqara, 2:25)

AS-SANI'
The Artificer; The Maker

You will see the mountains you reckoned to be solid going past like clouds—**the handiwork of Allah** Who gives to everything its solidity. He is aware of what you do. (Surat an-Naml, 27:88)

Every being, whether living or non-living, teems with signs of a superior wisdom and an infinite knowledge. No doubt, these manifest Allah's attribute of *al-'Aleem*. They also have another very important feature: a very delicate artistry. This attribute manifests itself in the form of an extraordinary appearance, flawlessness, a delicate and unique artistry, harmony, and design.

For instance, we can see the human body's flawless design. All organs are placed in the most appropriate place. For instance, the places of the eyes and the heart, the latter of which is protected by the sternum, are entrusted with many divine purposes. The body's symmetry, which is designed according to the "golden ratio" used by painters, is also strikingly beautiful. Indeed, each person's eyes, nose, and mouth are put into their individual places with great delicacy.

In many living beings, Allah created certain details to manifest His attribute of *as-Sani'*. As a result, every living being is unique. A tropical bird's wings or a flower's petals are dominated by phosphorous colors, whereas a butterfly's wings contain several colors. Similarly, a reptile, a bird, and a marine animal are totally different from each other.

This infinite artistry is also visible in the plant world. As **"And** also the things of varying colors He has created for you in the land. There is certainly a Sign in that for people who pay heed"** (Surat an-Nahl, 16:13) tells us, Allah created millions of different plants and flowers with various odors, smell, colors, and symmetry. For example, an orchid has hundreds of different appearances and colors. Similarly, a rose has many colors of varying tones. Such uniqueness is a clear sign of His artistry.

Allah manifests this attribute by presenting all of these aesthetic living beings to humanity. He could have created just one type of every living being. But by creating many species, He has displayed an amazing artistry that mere words cannot describe with full justice. Moreover, the examples of His artistry are wherever we look and are perfect.

AS-SALAM
The All-Peace

He is Allah—there is no deity but Him. He is the King, the Most Pure, **the Perfect Peace**, the Trustworthy, the Safeguarder, the Almighty, the Compeller, the Supremely Great. Glory be to Allah above all they associate with Him. (Surat al-Hashr, 59:23)

Allah gave the good news of an eternal Paradise to His believing servants. Yet one point is often missed here: These servants are rewarded with a beautiful life not only in the Hereafter but in this world as well, as the following verse reveals:

What is with you runs out, but what is with Allah goes on forever. Those who were steadfast will be recompensed according to the best of what they did. Anyone who acts rightly, male or female, being a believer, We will give them a good life and will recompense them according to the best of what they did. (Surat an-Nahl, 16:96-97)

No doubt, the blissful life in both worlds manifests Allah's attribute of *as-Salam* upon His faithful servants. A believer who is devoted to Allah and does good deeds to attain His good pleasure will return to His Lord "**...well pleasing and well pleased**" (Surat al-Fajr, 89:28). Allah describes what such servants will find in the Hereafter, as follows:

And the garden will be brought close to the pious not far away: "This is what you were promised. It is for every careful penitent: those who fear the All-Merciful in the Unseen and come with a contrite heart. Enter it in peace. This is the

Day of Timeless Eternity." They will have there everything they want, and with Us there is still more. (Surah Qaf, 50:31-35)

Allah's attribute of *as-Salam* is also His greeting to those who enter Paradise. In Surah Ya Sin 36:58 Allah states: "**'Peace!' A word from a Merciful Lord.**" This greeting is the greatest reward that believers will ever receive, for:

Such people will be repaid for their steadfastness with the Highest Paradise, where they will meet with welcome and with "Peace." (Surat al-Furqan, 25:75)

AS-SAMEE'
The All-Hearing

Certainly those who argue about the Signs of Allah without any authority having come to them have nothing in their hearts except pride, which they will never be able to vindicate. Therefore seek refuge with Allah. **He is the All-Hearing**, the All-Seeing. (Surah Ghafir, 40:56)

As well as seeing everything, Allah, Who is closer to us than our jugular veins, hears every noise in the universe. For example, He hears each noise made by all of the galaxies, planets, and celestial bodies; those made by the billions of invisible living beings living in the micro-universe, for He created them; and the noise made by a splitting seed, a flash of lightening, or a flying bird's wings. This fact is related in the following verse:

Say: "My Lord knows what is said in heaven and Earth. He is the All-Hearing, the All-Knowing." (Surat al-Anbiya', 21:4)

One sign of Allah's greatness and power is His hearing every noise made by all living and non-living beings. He hears—and answers—the prayers of all people who secretly turn to Him and call upon Him. Indeed, in another verse Allah states: **"If My servants ask you about Me, I am near. I answer the call of the caller when he calls upon Me..."** (Surat al-Baqara, 2:186). This is quite easy for Allah, for He is everywhere at the same moment.

In addition, Allah also hears the rebels' most delicate plots, for He encompasses all things in His knowledge. No person has ever uttered a single word without Him knowing it. They will be confronted by all of their words in the Hereafter, as the Qur'an reveals:

Say: "Do you worship, besides Allah, something that has no power to harm or help you when Allah is the All-Hearing, the All-Knowing?" (Surat al-Ma'ida, 5:76)

His Lord replied to him and turned away from him their female guile and deviousness. He is the One Who Hears, the One Who Knows. (Surah Yusuf, 12:34)

ASH-SHAFEE
The Affectionate; The Healer

And when I am ill, **it is He Who heals me.** (Surat ash-Shu'ara', 26:80)

Allah uses illness to force people to realize just how feeble they are and how much help they really need. Thus, the hundreds of diseases in our world are created for both bodily and spiritual purposes. For example, they are signs of a purposeful and superior creation and of His power, for how else can one explain the existence of microscopic viruses?

Only Allah can remove an illness, for He is the One Who created it. As a manifestation of *ash-Shafee*, Allah removes a disease whenever He wills. If He does not will this, no doctor, advanced technology, or innovative medication can help or cure the patient, for all medicine is only means of recovery. Each illness is sent so that we may ponder upon it, eventually see our Lord's infinite power next to our own feebleness, and seek His help whenever we are in distress. Believers have to be aware that Allah is their only guardian and helper.

The Qur'an praises Prophet Ayyub (as) for his submission to Allah. The moral excellence, patience, and trust he displayed in the face of devastating distress has become an example for all believers. The related verse is as follows:

And Ayyub, when he called out to his Lord: "Great harm has afflicted me, and You are the Most Merciful of the merciful." (Surat al-Anbiya', 21:83)

Allah answered his call and removed his distress, and Prophet Ayyub (as) earned the rewards of being patient and turning solely to Allah.

ASH-SHAFI'
The Intercessor

Or have they adopted intercessors besides Allah? Say: "Even though they do not control a thing and have no awareness?" Say: "**Intercession is entirely Allah's affair. The kingdom of the heavens and Earth is His. Then you will be returned to Him.**" (Surat az-Zumar, 39:43-44)

Those who have faith in Allah and yet associate partners with Him assume that these partners will intercede for them on the Day of Judgment. According to their belief, such "guardians" will take responsibility for their followers or purify them. And so they undertake strenuous efforts to earn their approval and constantly think of them. But this is no more than a huge delusion, for Allah states that He will be the only Protector on the Day of Judgment, as follows:

Abandon those who have turned their religion into a game and a diversion, who have been deluded by the life of the world. Remind [them] by it [the Qur'an], lest a person is delivered up to destruction for what he has earned with no protector or intercessor besides Allah. Were he to offer every kind of compensation, it would not be accepted from him... (Surat al-An'am, 6:70)

On that Day, no one will befriend another or bear someone's sins. As Allah informs us, only those who please Him will be allowed to intercede, and this person will surely say the truth. Unbelievers will find no guardian or intercessor on that Day, and no support, protection, or intercession, for Allah is the only Guardian and Intercessor:

Allah created the heavens and Earth and everything be-

tween them in six days, and then established Himself firmly upon the Throne. You have no protector or intercessor apart from Him. So will you not pay heed? (Surat as-Sajda, 32:4)

ASH-SHARIH
The Opener

Is he whose breast is opened to Islam, and who is therefore illuminated by his Lord...? Woe to those whose hearts are hardened against the remembrance of Allah! Such people are clearly misguided. (Surat az-Zumar, 39:22)

The existence of Allah and the Hereafter is obvious. Despite this, however, the majority of people have no faith. A person attains true faith only when Allah "opens one's breast to Islam." This acquisition of faith is the greatest blessing from Allah, for if Allah had no mercy and favor upon His sincere servants, none of them would attain salvation. While creating humanity, Allah gave every soul a lower self that would tempt each man and woman toward evil. However, He also ensured that His sincere servants could attain the straight path by both overcoming and avoiding such temptations.

This right path, which is attained by following one's conscience, is a blessing granted to sincere believers. As Allah informs us:

... However, Allah has given you love of faith and made it pleasing to your hearts, and has made disbelief, deviance, and disobedience hateful to you. People such as these are rightly guided. It is a great favor from Allah and a blessing. (Surat al-Hujurat, 49:7-8)

Those who forget how they were created and insist on unbelief, despite all of the signs surrounding them, who follow the dictates of their lower selves and do not exercise their conscience, will experience the following:

As for those who are unbelievers, it makes no difference to them whether you warn them or do not warn them; they will not believe. Allah has sealed up their hearts and hearing, and over their eyes is a blindfold. They will have a terrible punishment. (Surat al-Baqara, 2:6-7)

Have you seen him who takes his whims and desires to be his deity—whom Allah has misguided knowingly, sealing up his hearing and his heart and placing a blindfold over his eyes? Who, then, will guide him after Allah? So will you not pay heed? (Surat al-Jathiya, 45:23)

ASH-SHAHEED
The Witness

Say: "**Allah is a sufficient witness** between me and you. He is certainly aware of and sees His servants." (Surat al-Isra', 17:96)

Allah has no beginning and no end, is the sole absolute Being, and is not bound by such human concepts as time or space. Therefore, everything that ever happens, regardless of whether it happened in the past, the present, or the future, are the same in—and are fully known to—His Sight.

He knows everything, whether it is done in secret or in public, in darkness or in light, while alone or while in a crowd. Being ignorant, people assume that what they do at night might conceal their sins and hide them as well. But such hopes are futile, for the Qur'an states:

Do you not see that Allah knows what is in the heavens and on Earth? Three men cannot confer together secretly without Him being the fourth, or five without Him being the sixth, or fewer than that or more without Him being with them wherever they are. Then He will inform them on the Day of Rising of what they did. Allah has knowledge of all things. (Surat al-Mujadala, 58:7)

Allah is fully knowledgeable of everyone's intentions, thoughts, and deeds at every one moment. Each of us will be called to account for all of these on the Day of Judgment. People who deny these truths will understand their mistake on the Day of Judgment. As **"On the Day Allah raises up all of them together, He will in-**

form them of what they did. Allah has recorded it while they have forgotten it. Allah is a Witness of all things" (Surat al-Mujadala, 58:6) maintains, in the Hereafter we will be repaid for each one of our deeds:

You do not engage in any matter, recite any of the Qur'an, or do any action without Our witnessing you while you are occupied with it. Not even the smallest speck eludes your Lord, either on Earth or in heaven. Nor is there anything smaller than that, or larger, which is not in a Clear Book. (Surah Yunus, 10:61)

But Allah bears witness to what He has sent down to you. He has sent it down with His knowledge. The angels bear witness as well. And Allah suffices as a Witness. (Surat an-Nisa', 4:166)

Whether We show you something of what We have promised them or take you back to Us, they will still return to Us. Then Allah will be witness against what they are doing. (Surah Yunus, 10:46)

We will show them Our Signs on the horizon and within themselves until it is clear to them that it is the truth. Is it not enough for your Lord that He is a witness of everything? (Surah Fussilat, 41:53)

ASH-SHAKUR
The Appreciative; He Who Is Responsive to Gratitude

If you make a generous loan to Allah He will multiply it for you and forgive you. **Allah is most Ready to appreciate** [service], **Most Clement.** (Surat at-Taghabun, 64:17)

Allah gives countless blessings to us and only asks each of us to be a grateful servant. Allah draws our attention to the importance of being grateful in Surah Ibrahim 14:7: "**...And when your Lord announced: 'If you are grateful, I will certainly give you increase; but if you are ungrateful, My punishment is severe.'**"

One who does not give thanks for all of these blessings will be repaid in the Hereafter, for Allah's infinite justice requires this. However, Allah is very compassionate toward His servants, as the Qur'an states:

Allah does not wrong anyone by so much as the smallest speck. And if there is a good deed, Allah will multiply it and pay out an immense reward direct from Him. (Surat an-Nisa,' 4:40)

Whoever does a good deed for Allah's cause will be rewarded with what is better on the Day of Judgment.

That is the good news that Allah gives to His servants who believe and do right actions. Say: "I do not ask you for any wage for this—except for you to love your near of kin. If anyone does a good action, We will increase the good of it for him. Allah is Ever-Forgiving, Ever-Thankful." (Surat ash-Shura, 42:23)

That He will pay them their wages in full and give them more from His unbounded favor. He is Ever-Forgiving, Ever-Thankful. (Surah Fatir, 35:30)

They will say: "Praise be to Allah, Who has removed all sadness from us. Truly our Lord is Ever-Forgiving, Ever-Thankful." (Surah Fatir, 35:34)

AT-TAWWAB
The Acceptor of Repentance

Except for those who repent, put things right, and make things clear. I turn toward them. **I am the Ever-Returning, the Most Merciful.** (Surat al-Baqara, 2:160)

As stated earlier, humanity was created ignorant and ungrateful, and therefore is vulnerable to sins, mistakes, and weaknesses. This aside, Satan constantly tempts people and strives to plant vain desires and deviance in them. Yet, no matter how great one's mistakes and sins are, there is always a way out: sincere repentance and His ensuing forgiveness. For this reason, we should never lose hope, regardless of what we have done. In the Qur'an, Allah states:

Say: "My servants, you who have transgressed against yourselves, do not despair of the mercy of Allah. Truly Allah forgives all wrong actions. He is the Ever-Forgiving, the Most Merciful." (Surat az-Zumar, 39:53)

Meanwhile, there is a very important point we need to keep in mind:

Allah only accepts the repentance of those who do evil in ignorance and then quickly repent after doing it. Allah turns toward such people. Allah is All-Knowing, All-Wise. There is no repentance for people who persist in doing evil until death comes to them and who then say: "Now I repent," nor for people who die as unbelievers. We have prepared for them a painful punishment. (Surat an-Nisa', 4:17-18)

Clearly, Allah accepts the repentance of His sincere servants, for their regret and commitment to abandon their sinful behavior is real. Even clearer is the fact that the death-bed repentance of an unbeliever is meaningless. The Qur'an gives the example of the Pharaoh's insincere repentance:

> We brought the tribe of Israel across the sea, and Pharaoh and his troops pursued them out of tyranny and enmity. Then, when he was on the point of drowning, he said: "I believe that there is no deity but Him in whom the tribe of Israel believe. I am one of the Muslims." What, now! When previously you rebelled and were one of the corrupters? (Surah Yunus, 10:90-91)

> And also toward the three who were left behind, so that when the land became narrow for them, for all its great breadth, and their own selves became constricted for them and they realized that there was no refuge from Allah except in Him, He turned to them so that they might turn to Him. Allah is the Ever-Returning, the Most Merciful. (Surat at-Tawba, 9:118)

> Were it not for Allah's favor to you and His mercy ... and that Allah is Ever-Returning, All-Wise. (Surat an-Nur, 24:10)

AL-WAHID
The One

Your God is One God. There is no god but Him, the All-Merciful, the Most Merciful. (Surat al-Baqara, 2:163)

For centuries, people who have failed to grasp Allah's greatness have worshipped what they considered to be "superior" and "powerful" beings, such as the Sun or stars. Furthermore, despite all their feebleness, some people even dared to declare themselves as deities. In the Qur'an, Allah gives the example of a man who argued with Prophet Ibrahim (as) about Allah's unity and power. Prophet Ibrahim (as) responded in the following terms:

What about the one who argued with Ibrahim about his Lord, on the basis that Allah had given him sovereignty? Ibrahim said: "My Lord gives life and causes to die." He said: "I too give life and cause to die." Ibrahim said; "Allah makes the Sun come from the East. Make it come from the West." And the one who was an unbeliever was dumbfounded. Allah does not guide wrongdoing people. (Surat al-Baqara, 2:258)

Setting up any other deity with Allah is not unique to previous peoples, for we see it even in our own time. While modern people do not worship the Sun, particular stars, or similar items, they worship people who are just as helpless as themselves or such concepts as beauty, wealth, and power. They devote their lives to acquiring wealth and never once wonder if Allah is pleased with them. They consider people, other beings, or particular objects as equal to Allah and so clearly associate partners with Him.

Given that Allah is the Creator, no one can make the Sun rise from the West, stop the universe from expanding, hold the heavens and Earth, or create a human being from nothing. Allah is the only God, for nothing that exists can be equal to the Creator. The Qur'an describes the weakness of those who associate partners with Allah, as follows:

O mankind! An example has been made, so listen carefully. Those whom you call upon besides Allah cannot create a single fly, even if they were to join together to do it. And if a fly steals something from them, they cannot get it back. How feeble are both the seeker and the sought! (Surat al-Hajj, 22:73)

... Or have they assigned partners to Allah who create as He creates, so that all creating seems the same to them? Say: "Allah is the Creator of everything. He is the One, the All-Conquering."(Surat ar-Ra'd, 13:16)

... The Messiah, 'Isa son of Maryam, was only the Messenger of Allah and His Word, which He cast into Maryam, and a Spirit from Him. So believe in Allah and His Messengers. Do not say: "Three." It is better that you stop. Allah is only One God. He is too Glorious to have a son! Everything in the heavens and in Earth belongs to Him. Allah suffices as a Guardian. (Surat an-Nisa', 4:171)

AL-WARITH
The Inheritor

How many cities We have destroyed that lived in insolent ingratitude! There are their houses, never again inhabited after them, except a little. **It was We Who were their Heir.** (Surat al-Qasas, 28:58)

Throughout their lives, such people strive to accumulate more wealth. Some people are so committed to this end that this goal takes over their lives and leaves them no time to wonder why they exist. However, there is one fact these people disregard:

Say: "Shall I inform you of the greatest losers in their actions? People whose efforts in the life of the world are misguided while they suppose that they are doing good." (Surat al-Kahf, 18:103-04)

Indeed, until their last breath, they strive for a vain purpose. Yet one day, at a totally unexpected moment, they will face the angels of death. Wrapped in a simple shroud, these people, who were widely admired because of their wealth, will be buried in the ground and thus leave everything behind. All they can take with them into their graves is their naked body, their fear, and their closeness to Allah.

Allah is the sole Inheritor of Earth, and His sincere servants are made wealthy by His favor. As we mentioned above, all wealth, status, and respect enjoyed in this world is temporary. Allah, Who grants all of these blessings, takes each person's soul whenever He wills. The Qur'an reveals how each person will be brought before Allah's presence:

We give life and cause to die, and We are the Inheritor.

(Surat al-Hijr, 15:23)

And Zakariyya, when he called out to his Lord: "My Lord, do not leave me on my own, though You are the Best of Inheritors." (Surat al-Anbiya', 21:89)

AL-WASI'
The All-Embracing; The Boundless

O You who believe! If any of you renounce your religion, Allah will bring forward a people whom He loves and who love Him, humble to the believers, fierce to the unbelievers, who strive in the Way of Allah and do not fear the blame of any censurer. That is the unbounded favor of Allah, which He gives to whoever He wills. **Allah is Boundless,** All-Knowing. (Surat al-Ma'ida, 5:54)

Allah encompasses all universes. As the Creator of everything Who is not bound by place, He is above all places. In many societies, people commonly believe that Allah resides in the heavens. Thus, while calling upon him, they turn their faces to the heavens. The fact is, however, that **"Both East and West belong to Allah, so wherever you turn, the Face of Allah is there. Allah is All-Encompassing, All-Knowing."**(Surat al-Baqara, 2:115)

Allah informs us that He is the Lord of the heavens and Earth. Given this, He clearly settled Himself everywhere and owns everything that exists. His blessings never end, His mercy is boundless, His forgiveness is vast, and His mercy and compassion are infinite. Allah's attribute of *al-Wasi* manifests itself especially on believers. As His mercy and compassion are vast, He encompasses His faithful servants with His mercy and protects them. For instance, some unbelievers seek to harm religion by imposing hardships, such as by saying, **"... Do not spend on those who are with the Messenger of Allah, so that they may go away..."** (Surat al-Munafiqun, 63:7). But all of these efforts are futile, for Allah gives His unbounded mercy and wealth to whomever He wills, for He owns the treasures of the heavens and Earth. One verse mentions that He is All-Encompassing:

> [A group of the People of the Book say,] "Do not trust anyone, except for those who follow your religion." Say: "Allah's guidance is true guidance. But you think it is impossible for anyone to be given the same as you were given, or to argue with you before your Lord." Say: "All favor is in Allah's Hand, and He gives it to whoever He wills. Allah is All-Encompassing, All-Knowing." (Surah Al 'Imran, 3:73)

AL-WADUD
The Loving

He is the Ever-Forgiving, **the All-Loving**. (Surat al-Buruj, 85:14)

Those people who understand that Allah created humanity to serve Him remain sincere to Him until they die, while others deny His existence. Allah is very close to His loyal servants. He hears and answers their prayers, is with them whenever they encounter a difficulty, and supports them at every stage of their lives.

One of the greatest blessings that people may attain in this life is Allah's love and friendship. Allah's beloved servants lead honorable and distinguished lives, and their moral perfection always earns great admiration and appreciation. He admits His beloved servants into His mercy and lets them enter Paradise. Prophets and sincere believers are very valuable people who have earned Allah's love, love Allah, and lead their lives only to earn His good pleasure.

Ask your Lord for forgiveness, and then repent to Him. My Lord is Most Merciful, Most Loving. (Surah Hud, 11:90)

AL-WAHHAB
The All-Giving

Or do they possess the treasuries of your Lord's mercy, the Almighty, **the Ever-Giving?** (Surah Sad, 38:9)

Allah promised a life of infinite happiness in Paradise, which starts here in this world, for He also promised a beautiful life in this world. This is why sincere believers see no limits when asking their Lord to meet their needs. They can ask their Lord for anything that will draw them nearer to Him. Allah answers these calls as He wills, and His answer is always the best. One example is Prophet Sulayman's (as) prayer: **"Truly do I love the love of good, with a view to the glory of my Lord"** (Surah Sad, 38:32) and continued:

He said: "My Lord, forgive me and give me a kingdom the like of which will never be granted to anyone after me. Truly You are the Ever-Giving." (Surah Sad, 38:35)

Prophet Sulayman (as) prayed for such a kingdom because he knew that Allah rewards His sincere servants both in this world and in the Hereafter. One verse reads:

Our Lord, do not make our hearts swerve aside after You have guided us. And give us mercy from You. You are the Ever-Giving. (Surah Al 'Imran, 3:8)

AL-WAKEEL
The Guardian

They have the word "obedience" on their tongues, but when they leave your presence, a group of them spend the night plotting to do other than what you say. Allah is recording their nocturnal plotting. So let them be and put your trust in Allah. **Allah suffices as a Guardian.** (Surat an-Nisa', 4:81)

Allah wants His sincere and faithful servants to trust Him in every circumstance. Indeed, all Prophets encountered many difficulties and much enmity while spreading Allah's message within their unbelieving communities. And yet they always maintained their brave and resolute attitude for, seeking only Allah's good pleasure, they took refuge in Allah.

Allah informs us that He helps those who help His religion. There will always be people who fight believers and follow Satan. They may hatch plots to harm believers and strive to break their zeal with offensive words and slanders. Yet they can never attain their goals, for their plans are feeble next to Allah's infinite power and wisdom. Allah, Who knows and sees all the details of every plot, helps the patient and resolute believers who befriend Him and enables them to attain the best. This metaphysical phenomenon is incomprehensible to unbelievers. In this way, believers who trust in Allah attain great spiritual and physical strength. Allah mentions this in the following verses:

Those who submit themselves completely to Allah and do good have grasped the Firmest Handhold. The end result of all affairs is with Allah. (Surah Luqman, 31:22)

Those to whom people said: "The people have gathered against you, so fear them." But that merely increased their faith, and they said: "Allah is enough for us and the Best of Guardians." (Surah Al 'Imran, 3:173)

Taking Allah as their guardian has always resulted in their victory. The related verses read:

So they returned with blessings and bounty from Allah, and no evil touched them. They pursued the pleasure of Allah. Allah's favor is indeed immense. (Surah Al 'Imran, 3:174)

Lord of the East and West—there is no deity but Him—so take Him as your Guardian. (Surat al-Muzzammil, 73:9)

Say: "Nothing can happen to us except what Allah has ordained for us. He is Our Master. It is in Allah that the believers should put their trust." (Surat at-Tawba, 9:51)

AL-WALEE
The Protector

Allah is the Protector of those who believe. He brings them out of the darkness and into the light. But those who do not believe have false deities as protectors. They take them from the light into the darkness. Those are the Companions of the Fire remaining in it timelessly, forever. (Surat al-Baqara, 2:257)

Both in this world and in the next, people have only one real friend. This friend never abandons them, is next to them, and helps them in the face of every difficulty. From the day they are born until they die, He is always with them and protects them against their enemies. He is more reliable than anyone else, and always rewards them without expecting anything in return. This friend, of course, is our Lord, the believers' most intimate friend, Who purifies all those who place their trust in Him and promise them a distinguished life here and eternal wealth in the Hereafter.

Throughout their lives, people seek someone more powerful or wealthier upon whom they can rely in all circumstances. Yet while seeking such people, they totally forget our All-Mighty Lord, Who created them and meets all of their needs. They take Satan, who only leads them toward sin and hinders them from attaining Paradise, as their friend. This is the beginning of a gloomy world.

People who have faith and sincere faith in Allah, on the other hand, enjoy a good and honorable life. In this life, there is no room for failure, because Allah grants victory to believers as long as they remain committed to their religion and their words. Meanwhile, the actual reward is waiting for them in the Hereafter. Allah is the sole real protector of believers both in this world and beyond. His attribute of *al-Walee* is described in the following verses:

> **Allah knows best who your enemies are. Allah suffices as a Protector; Allah suffices as a Helper. (Surat an-Nisa', 4:45)**
>
> **And remember when two of your clans were on the point of losing heart and Allah was their Protector. Let the believers put their trust in Allah. (Surah Al 'Imran, 3:122)**
>
> **It is He Who sends down abundant rain, after they have lost all hope, and unfolds His mercy. He is the Protector, the Praiseworthy. (Surat ash-Shura, 42:28)**

DHU AL-JALAL WA AL-IKRAM
Master of Majesty and Generosity

Blessed be the name of your Lord, Master of Majesty and Generosity. (Surat ar-Rahman, 55:78)

People enjoy countless blessings, for Allah has adorned this world with many details that are pleasing to His servants. However, Allah will show His infinite generosity in Paradise.

One of the most telling attributes of the Paradise is that believers will have all that their hearts desire, without any limit. There will be gardens with rivers flowing underneath and cool, refreshing shade. By the grace of Allah, devout believers will be amid shaded gardens with spreading branched, flowing springs, and whatever kind of fruit and meat they desire. In addition, they will have high-ceilinged halls with rivers flowing underneath, where they will recline on couches ranged in rows and take pleasure from the surrounding beauty. Circulating among them will be youths like hidden pearls, passing among them vessels of silver and goblets of pure crystal. Meanwhile, "... they will be adorned with gold bracelets and pearls, and where their clothing will be of silk." (Surat al-Hajj, 22:23)

No doubt, the Qur'an's descriptions of Paradise are far more elaborate than what we could convey above. The verses below give a detailed description of Allah's infinite generosity in Paradise:

... they will have there all that their hearts desire and their eyes find delight in. You will remain in it timelessly, forever. (Surat az-Zukhruf, 43:71)

Seeing them, you see delight and a great kingdom. (Surat al-Insan, 76:20)

AZ-ZAHIR
The Evident; The Outward

He is the First and the Last, **the Outward** and the Inward. He has knowledge of all things. (Surat al-Hadid, 57:3)

The signs of Allah's existence, which are spread throughout the universe, are evident for all people of understanding. Grasping Allah's existence demands no more than a careful scrutiny into one's surroundings, for the universe abounds with signs of creation. From the simplest to the most complex ones, all systems reveal a network of miracles that present even more mysteries as one makes an in-depth analysis. In the Qur'an, Allah gives the following examples of these miracles:

Have they not looked at the sky above them: how We structured it and made it beautiful, and how there are no fissures in it? And Earth: how We stretched it out and cast firmly embedded mountains onto it and caused luxuriant plants of every kind to grow in it? (Surah Qaf, 50:6-7)

Have they not looked at the birds above them, with wings outspread and folded back? Nothing holds them up but the All-Merciful. He sees all things. (Surat al-Mulk, 67:19)

Allah splits the seed and kernel. He brings forth the living from the dead, and produces the dead out of the living. That is Allah, so how are you deluded? He splits the sky at dawn, and appoints the night as a time of stillness and the Sun and the Moon as a means of reckoning. That is what the Almighty, the All-Knowing has ordained. He has appointed the stars for you so you might be guided by them

in the darkness of the land and sea. We have made the Signs clear for people who have knowledge. (Surat al-An'am, 6:95-97)

No doubt, these are just a few examples. Elsewhere, Allah reminds His servants of His existence through many examples. One of their most telling attributes is that they ponder over everything they see and gradually comprehend Allah's existence and greatness. As we mentioned above, each detail in our universe makes us feel that we were created.

People of intelligence who recognize Allah's greatness and power surely feel an inner awe toward our Creator, Who will call each one of them to account for their deeds in the Hereafter. Therefore, they spend their lives striving to earn His good pleasure. In one verse, Allah says the following:

Those who remember Allah, standing, sitting, and lying on their sides, and reflect on the creation of the heavens and Earth: "Our Lord, You have not created this for nothing. Glory be to You! So safeguard us from the punishment of the Fire." (Surah Al 'Imran, 3:191)

THE DECEPTION OF EVOLUTION

Darwinism, in other words the theory of evolution, was put forward with the aim of denying the fact of creation, but is in truth nothing but failed, unscientific nonsense. This theory, which claims that life emerged by chance from inanimate matter, was invalidated by the scientific evidence of clear "design" in the universe and in living things. In this way, science confirmed the fact that Allah created the universe and the living things in it. The propaganda carried out today in order to keep the theory of evolution alive is based solely on the distortion of the scientific facts, biased interpretation, and lies and falsehoods disguised as science.

Yet this propaganda cannot conceal the truth. The fact that the theory of evolution is the greatest deception in the history of science has been expressed more and more in the scientific world over the last 20-30 years. Research carried out after the 1980s in particular has revealed that the claims of Darwinism are totally unfounded, something that has been stated by a large number of scientists. In the United States in particular, many scientists from such different fields as biology, biochemistry and paleontology recognize the invalidity of Darwinism and employ the concept of intelligent design to account for the origin of life. This "intelligent design" is a scientific expression of the fact that Allah created all living things.

We have examined the collapse of the theory of evolution and the proofs of creation in great scientific detail in many of our works, and are still continuing to do so. Given the enormous importance of this subject, it will be of great benefit to summarize it here.

THE SCIENTIFIC COLLAPSE OF DARWINISM

Although this doctrine goes back as far as ancient Greece, the theory of evolution was advanced extensively in the nineteenth century. The most important development that made it the top topic of the world of science was Charles Darwin's *The Origin of Species*, published in 1859. In this book, he denied that Allah created different living species on Earth separately, for he claimed that all living beings had a common ancestor and had diversified over time through small changes. Darwin's theory was not based on any concrete scientific finding; as he also accepted, it was just an "assumption." Moreover, as Darwin confessed in the long chapter of his book titled "Difficulties of the Theory," the theory failed in the face of many critical questions.

Darwin invested all of his hopes in new scientific discoveries, which he expected to solve these difficulties. However, contrary to his expectations, scientific findings expanded the dimensions of these difficulties. The defeat of Darwinism in the face of science can be reviewed under three basic topics:

1) The theory cannot explain how life originated on Earth.

2) No scientific finding shows that the "evolutionary mechanisms" proposed by the theory have any evolutionary power at all.

3) The fossil record proves the exact opposite of what the theory suggests.

In this section, we will examine these three basic points in general outlines:

THE FIRST INSURMOUNTABLE STEP: THE ORIGIN OF LIFE

The theory of evolution posits that all living species evolved from a single living cell that emerged on the primitive Earth 3.8 billion years ago. How a single cell could generate millions of complex living species and, if such an evolution really occurred, why traces of it cannot be observed in the fossil record are some of the questions that the theory cannot answer. However, first and foremost, we need to ask: How did this "first cell" originate?

Since the theory of evolution denies creation and any kind of supernatural intervention, it maintains that the "first cell" originated coincidentally within the laws of nature, without any design, plan or arrangement. According to the theory, inanimate matter must have produced a living cell as a result of coincidences. Such a claim, however, is inconsistent with the most unassailable rules of biology.

"LIFE COMES FROM LIFE"

In his book, Darwin never referred to the origin of life. The primitive understanding of science in his time rested on the assumption that living beings had a very simple structure. Since medieval times, spontaneous generation, which asserts that non-living materials came together to form living organisms, had been widely accepted. It was commonly believed that insects came into being from food leftovers, and mice from wheat. Interesting experiments were conducted to prove this theory. Some wheat was placed on a dirty piece of cloth, and it was believed that mice would originate from it after a while.

Similarly, maggots developing in rotting meat was assumed to be evidence of spontaneous generation. However, it was later understood that worms did not appear on meat spontaneously, but were carried there by flies in the form of larvae, invisible to the naked eye.

Even when Darwin wrote *The Origin of Species*, the belief that bacteria could come into existence from non-living matter was widely accepted in the world of science.

However, five years after the publication of Darwin's book, Louis Pasteur announced his results after long studies and experiments, that disproved spontaneous generation, a cornerstone of Darwin's theory. In his triumphal lecture at the Sorbonne in 1864, Pasteur said: "Never will the doctrine of spontaneous generation recover from the mortal blow struck by this simple experiment."[1]

For a long time, advocates of the theory of evolution resisted these findings. However, as the development of science unraveled the complex structure of the cell of a living being, the idea that life could come into being coincidentally faced an even greater impasse.

INCONCLUSIVE EFFORTS IN THE TWENTIETH CENTURY

The first evolutionist who took up the subject of the origin of life in the twentieth century was the renowned Russian biologist Alexander Oparin. With various theses he advanced in the 1930s, he tried to prove that a living cell could originate by coincidence. These studies, however, were doomed to failure, and Oparin had to make the following confession:

Unfortunately, however, the problem of the origin of the cell is perhaps the most obscure point in the whole study of the evolution of organisms.[2]

Evolutionist followers of Oparin tried to carry out experiments to solve this problem. The best known experiment was carried out by the American chemist Stanley Miller in 1953. Combining the gases he alleged to have existed in the primordial Earth's atmosphere in an experiment set-up, and adding energy to the mixture, Miller synthesized several organic molecules (amino acids) present in the structure of proteins.

Barely a few years had passed before it was revealed that this experiment, which was then presented as an important step in the name of evolution, was invalid, for the atmosphere used in the experiment was very different from the real Earth conditions.[3]

After a long silence, Miller confessed that the atmosphere medium he used was unrealistic.[4]

All the evolutionists' efforts throughout the twentieth century to explain the origin of life ended in failure. The geochemist Jeffrey Bada, from the San Diego Scripps Institute accepts this fact in an article published in *Earth* magazine in 1998:

Today as we leave the twentieth century, we still face the biggest unsolved problem that we had when we entered the twentieth century: How did life originate on Earth?[5]

THE COMPLEX STRUCTURE OF LIFE

The primary reason why the theory of evolution ended up in such a great impasse regarding the origin of life is that even those living organisms deemed to be the simplest have incredibly complex structures. The cell of a living thing is more complex than all of our man-made technological products. Today, even in the most developed laboratories of the world, a living cell cannot be produced by bringing organic chemicals together.

The conditions required for the formation of a cell are too great in quantity to be explained away by coincidences. The probability of proteins, the building blocks of a cell, being synthesized coincidentally, is 1 in 10^{950} for an average protein made up of 500 amino acids. In mathematics, a probability smaller than 1 over 10^{50} is considered to be impossible in practical terms.

The DNA molecule, which is located in the nucleus of a cell and which stores genetic information, is an incredible databank. If the information coded in DNA were written down, it would make a giant library consisting of an estimated 900 volumes of encyclopedias consisting of 500 pages each.

A very interesting dilemma emerges at this point: DNA can replicate itself only with the help of some specialized proteins (enzymes). However, the synthesis of these enzymes can be realized only by the information coded in DNA. As they both depend on each other, they have to exist at the same time for replication. This brings the scenario that life originated by itself to a deadlock. Prof. Leslie Orgel, an evolutionist of repute from the University of San Diego, California, confesses this fact in the September 1994 issue of the *Scientific American* magazine:

It is extremely improbable that proteins and nucleic acids, both of which are structurally complex, arose spontaneously in the same place at the same time. Yet it also seems impossible to have one without the other. And so, at first glance, one might have to conclude that life could never, in fact, have originated by chemical means.[6]

No doubt, if it is impossible for life to have originated from natural causes, then it has to be accepted that life was "created" in a supernatural way. This fact explicitly invalidates the theory of evolution, whose main purpose is to deny creation.

IMAGINARY MECHANISM OF EVOLUTION

The second important point that negates Darwin's theory is that both concepts put forward by the theory as "evolutionary mechanisms" were understood to have, in reality, no evolutionary power.

Darwin based his evolution allegation entirely on the mechanism of "natural selection." The importance he placed on this mechanism was evident in the name of his book: *The Origin of Species, By Means of Natural Selection...*

Natural selection holds that those living things that are stronger and more suited to the natural conditions of their habitats will survive in the struggle for life. For example, in a deer herd under the threat of attack by wild animals, those that can run faster will survive. Therefore, the deer herd will be comprised of faster and stronger individuals. However, unquestionably, this mechanism will not cause deer to evolve and transform themselves into another living species, for instance, horses.

Therefore, the mechanism of natural selection has no evolutionary power. Darwin was also aware of this fact and had to state this in his book *The Origin of Species*:

Natural selection can do nothing until favorable individual differences or variations occur.[7]

LAMARCK'S IMPACT

So, how could these "favorable variations" occur? Darwin tried to answer this question from the standpoint of the primitive understanding of science at that time. According to the French biologist Chevalier de Lamarck (1744-1829), who lived before Darwin, living creatures passed on the traits they acquired during their lifetime to the next generation. He asserted that these traits, which accumulated from one generation to another, caused new species to be formed. For instance, he claimed that giraffes evolved from antelopes; as they struggled to eat the leaves of high trees, their necks were extended from generation to generation.

Darwin also gave similar examples. In his book *The Origin of Species*, for instance, he said that some bears going into water to find food transformed themselves into whales over time.[8]

However, the laws of inheritance discovered by Gregor Mendel (1822-84) and verified by the science of genetics, which flourished in the twentieth century, utterly demolished the legend that acquired traits were passed on to subsequent generations. Thus, natural selection fell out of favor as an evolutionary mechanism.

NEO-DARWINISM AND MUTATIONS

In order to find a solution, Darwinists advanced the "Modern Synthetic Theory," or as it is more commonly known, Neo-Darwinism, at the end of the 1930's. Neo-Darwinism added mutations, which are distortions formed in the genes of living beings due to such external factors as radiation or replication errors, as the "cause of favorable variations" in addition to natural mutation.

Today, the model that stands for evolution in the world is Neo-Darwinism. The theory maintains that millions of living beings formed as a result of a process whereby numerous complex organs of these organisms (e.g., ears, eyes, lungs, and wings) underwent "mutations," that is, genetic disorders. Yet, there is an outright scientific fact that totally undermines this theory: Mutations do not cause living beings to develop; on the contrary, they are always harmful.

The reason for this is very simple: DNA has a very complex structure, and random effects can only harm it. The American geneticist B. G. Ranganathan explains this as follows:

First, genuine mutations are very rare in nature. Secondly, most mutations are harmful since they are random, rather than orderly changes in the structure of genes; any random change in a highly ordered system will be for the worse, not for the better. For example, if an earthquake were to shake a highly ordered structure such as a building, there would be a random change in the framework of the building which, in all probability, would not be an improvement.[9]

Not surprisingly, no mutation example, which is useful, that is, which is observed to develop the genetic code, has been observed so far. All mutations have proved to be harmful. It was understood that mutation, which is presented as an "evolutionary mechanism," is actually a genetic occurrence that harms living things, and leaves them disabled. (The most common effect of mutation on human beings is cancer.) Of course, a destructive mechanism cannot be an "evolutionary mechanism." Natural selection, on the other hand, "can do nothing by itself," as Darwin also accepted. This fact shows us that there is no "evolutionary mechanism" in nature. Since no evolutionary mechanism exists, no such any imaginary process called "evolution" could have taken place.

THE FOSSIL RECORD: NO SIGN OF INTERMEDIATE FORMS

The clearest evidence that the scenario suggested by the theory of evolution did not take place is the fossil record.

According to this theory, every living species has sprung from a predecessor. A previously existing species turned into something else over time and all species have come into being in this way. In other words, this transformation proceeds gradually over millions of years.

Had this been the case, numerous intermediary species should have existed and lived within this long transformation period.

For instance, some half-fish/half-reptiles should have lived in the past which had acquired some reptilian traits in addition to the fish traits they already had. Or there should have existed some reptile-birds, which acquired some bird traits in addition to the reptilian traits they already had. Since these would be in a transitional phase, they should be disabled, defective, crippled living beings. Evolutionists refer to these imaginary creatures, which they believe to have lived in the past, as "transitional forms."

If such animals ever really existed, there should be millions and even billions of them in number and variety. More importantly, the remains of these strange creatures should be present in the fossil record. In *The Origin of Species*, Darwin explained:

> If my theory be true, numberless intermediate varieties, linking most closely all of the species of the same group together must assuredly have existed... Consequently, evidence of their former existence could be found only amongst fossil remains.[10]

DARWIN'S HOPES SHATTERED

However, although evolutionists have been making strenuous efforts to find fossils since the middle of the nineteenth century all over the world, no transitional forms have yet been uncovered. All of the fossils, contrary to the evolutionists' expectations, show that life appeared on Earth all of a sudden and fully-formed.

One famous British paleontologist, Derek V. Ager, admits this fact, even though he is an evolutionist:

The point emerges that if we examine the fossil record in detail, whether at the level of orders or of species, we find—over and over again—not gradual evolution, but the sudden explosion of one group at the expense of another.[11]

This means that in the fossil record, all living species suddenly emerge as fully formed, without any intermediate forms in between. This is just the opposite of Darwin's assumptions. Also, this is very strong evidence that all living things are created. The only explanation of a living species emerging suddenly and complete in every detail without any evolutionary ancestor is that it was created. This fact is admitted also by the widely known evolutionist biologist Douglas Futuyma:

Creation and evolution, between them, exhaust the possible explanations for the origin of living things. Organisms either appeared on the earth fully developed or they did not. If they did not, they must have developed from pre-existing species by some process of modification. If they did appear in a fully developed state, they must indeed have been created by some omnipotent intelligence.[12]

Fossils show that living beings emerged fully developed and in a perfect state on the Earth. That means that "the origin of species," contrary to Darwin's supposition, is not evolution, but creation.

THE TALE OF HUMAN EVOLUTION

The subject most often brought up by advocates of the theory of evolution is the subject of the origin of man. The Darwinist claim holds that modern man evolved from ape-like creatures. During this alleged evolutionary process, which is supposed to have started 4-5 million years ago, some "transitional forms" between modern man and his ancestors are supposed to have existed. According to this completely imaginary scenario, four basic "categories" are listed:

1. *Australopithecus*
2. *Homo habilis*
3. *Homo erectus*
4. *Homo sapiens*

Evolutionists call man's so-called first ape-like ancestors *Australopithecus*, which means "South African ape." These living beings are actually nothing but an old ape species that has become extinct. Extensive research done on various *Australopithecus* specimens by two world famous anatomists from England and the USA, namely, Lord Solly Zuckerman and Prof. Charles Oxnard, shows that these apes belonged to an ordinary ape species that became extinct and bore no resemblance to humans.[13]

Evolutionists classify the next stage of human evolution as "homo," that is "man." According to their claim, the living beings in the *Homo* series are more developed than *Australopithecus*. Evolutionists devise a fanciful evolution scheme by arranging different fossils of these creatures in a particular order. This scheme is imaginary because it has never been proved that there is an evolutionary relation between these different classes. Ernst Mayr, one of the twentieth century's most important evolutionists, contends in his book *One Long Argument* that "particularly historical [puzzles] such as the origin of life or of *Homo sapiens*, are extremely difficult and may even resist a final, satisfying explanation."[14]

By outlining the link chain as *Australopithecus* > *Homo habilis* > *Homo erectus* > *Homo sapiens*, evolutionists imply that each of these species is one another's ancestor. However, recent findings of paleoanthropologists have revealed that *Australopithecus*, *Homo habilis*, and *Homo erectus* lived at different parts of the world at the same time.[15]

Moreover, a certain segment of humans classified as *Homo erectus* have lived up until very modern times. *Homo sapiens neandarthalensis* and *Homo sapiens sapiens* (modern man) co-existed in the same region.[16]

This situation apparently indicates the invalidity of the claim that they are ancestors of one another. A paleontologist from Harvard University, Stephen Jay Gould, explains this deadlock of the theory of evolution, although he is an evolutionist himself:

What has become of our ladder if there are three coexisting lineages of hominids (*A. africanus*, the robust australopithecines, and *H. habilis*), none clearly derived from another? Moreover, none of the three display any evolutionary trends during their tenure on earth.[17]

Put briefly, the scenario of human evolution, which is "upheld" with the help of various drawings of some "half ape, half human" creatures appearing in the media and course books, that is, frankly, by means of propaganda, is nothing but a tale with no scientific foundation.

Lord Solly Zuckerman, one of the most famous and respected scientists in the U.K., who carried out research on this subject for years and studied *Australopithecus* fossils for 15 years, finally concluded, despite being an evolutionist himself, that there is, in fact, no such family tree branching out from ape-like creatures to man.

Zuckerman also made an interesting "spectrum of science" ranging from those he considered scientific to those he considered unscientific. According to Zuckerman's spectrum, the most "scientific"—that is, depending on concrete data—fields of science are chemistry and physics. After them come the biological sciences and then the social sciences. At the far end of the spectrum, which is the part considered to be most "unscientific," are "extra-sensory perception"—concepts such as telepathy and sixth sense—and finally "human evolution." Zuckerman explains his reasoning:

> We then move right off the register of objective truth into those fields of presumed biological science, like extrasensory perception or the interpretation of man's fossil history, where to the faithful [evolutionist] anything is possible—and where the ardent believer [in evolution] is sometimes able to believe several contradictory things at the same time.[18]

The tale of human evolution boils down to nothing but the prejudiced interpretations of some fossils unearthed by certain people, who blindly adhere to their theory.

DARWINIAN FORMULA!

Besides all the technical evidence we have dealt with so far, let us now for once, examine what kind of a superstition the evolutionists have with an example so simple as to be understood even by children:

The theory of evolution asserts that life is formed by chance. According to this claim, lifeless and unconscious atoms came together to form the cell and then they somehow formed other living things, including man. Let us think about that. When we bring together the elements that are the building-blocks of life such as carbon, phosphorus, nitrogen and potassium, only a heap is formed. No matter what treatments it undergoes, this atomic heap cannot form even a single living being. If you like, let us formulate an "experiment" on this subject and let us examine on the behalf of evolutionists what they really claim without pronouncing loudly under the name "Darwinian formula":

Let evolutionists put plenty of materials present in the composition of living things such as phosphorus, nitrogen, carbon, oxygen, iron, and magnesium into big barrels. Moreover, let them add in these barrels any material that does not exist under normal conditions, but they think as necessary. Let them add in this mixture as many amino acids—which have no possibility of forming under natural conditions—and as many proteins—a single one of which has a formation probability of 10^{-950}—as they like. Let them expose these mixtures to as much heat and moisture as they like. Let them stir these with whatever technologically developed device they like. Let them put the foremost scientists beside these barrels. Let these experts wait in turn beside these barrels for billions, and even trillions of years. Let them be free to use all kinds of conditions they believe to be necessary for a human's formation. No matter what they do, they cannot produce from these barrels a human, say a professor that examines his cell structure under the electron microscope. They cannot produce giraffes, lions, bees, canaries, horses, dolphins, roses, orchids, lilies, carnations, bananas, oranges, apples, dates, tomatoes, melons, watermelons, figs, olives, grapes, peaches, peafowls, pheasants, multicoloured butterflies, or millions of other living beings such as these. Indeed, they could not obtain even a single cell of any one of them.

Briefly, unconscious atoms cannot form the cell by coming together. They cannot take a new decision and divide this cell into two, then take other decisions and create the professors who first invent the electron microscope and then examine their own cell structure under that microscope. Matter is an unconscious, lifeless heap, and it comes to life with Allah's superior creation.

The theory of evolution, which claims the opposite, is a total fallacy completely contrary to reason. Thinking even a little bit on the claims of evolutionists discloses this reality, just as in the above example.

TECHNOLOGY IN THE EYE AND THE EAR

Another subject that remains unanswered by evolutionary theory is the excellent quality of perception in the eye and the ear.

Before passing on to the subject of the eye, let us briefly answer the question of how we see. Light rays coming from an object fall oppositely on the eye's retina. Here, these light rays are transmitted into electric signals by cells and reach a tiny spot at the back of the brain, the "center of vision." These electric signals are perceived in this center as an image after a series of processes. With this technical background, let us do some thinking.

The brain is insulated from light. That means that its inside is completely dark, and that no light reaches the place where it is located. Thus, the "center of vision" is never touched by light and may even be the darkest place you have ever known. However, you observe a luminous, bright world in this pitch darkness.

The image formed in the eye is so sharp and distinct that even the technology of the twentieth century has not been able to attain it. For instance, look at the book you are reading, your hands with which you are holding it, and then lift your head and look around you. Have you ever seen such a sharp and distinct image as this one at any other place? Even the most developed television screen produced by the greatest television producer in the world cannot provide such a sharp image for you. This is a three-dimensional, colored, and extremely sharp image. For more than 100 years, thousands of engineers have been trying to achieve this sharpness. Factories, huge premises were established, much research has been done, plans and designs have been made for this purpose. Again, look at a TV screen and the book you hold in your hands. You will see that there is a big difference in sharpness and distinction. Moreover, the TV screen shows you a two-dimensional image, whereas with your eyes, you watch a three-dimensional perspective with depth.

For many years, tens of thousands of engineers have tried to make a three-dimensional TV and achieve the vision quality of the eye. Yes, they have made a three-dimensional television system, but it is not possible to watch it without putting on special 3-D glasses; moreover, it is only an artificial three-dimension. The background is more blurred, the foreground appears like a paper setting. Never has it been possible to produce a sharp and distinct vision like that of the eye. In both the camera and the television, there is a loss of image quality.

Evolutionists claim that the mechanism producing this sharp and distinct image has been formed by chance. Now, if somebody told you that the television in your room was formed as a result of chance, that all of its atoms just happened to come together and make up this device that produces an image, what would you think? How can atoms do what thousands of people cannot?

If a device producing a more primitive image than the eye could not have been formed by chance, then it is very evident that the eye and the image seen by the eye could not have been formed by chance. The same situation applies to the ear. The outer ear picks up the available sounds by the auricle and directs them to the middle ear, the middle ear transmits the sound vibrations by intensifying them, and the inner ear sends these vibrations to the brain by translating them into electric signals. Just as with the eye, the act of hearing finalizes in the center of hearing in the brain.

The situation in the eye is also true for the ear. That is, the brain is insulated from sound just as it is from light. It does not let any sound in. Therefore, no matter how noisy is the outside, the inside of the brain is completely silent. Nevertheless, the sharpest sounds are perceived in the brain. In your completely silent brain, you listen to symphonies, and hear all of the noises in a crowded place. However, were the sound level in your brain was measured by a precise device at that moment, complete silence would be found to be prevailing there.

As is the case with imagery, decades of effort have been spent in trying to generate and reproduce sound that is faithful to the original. The results of these efforts are sound recorders, high-fidelity systems, and systems for sensing sound. Despite all of this technology and the thousands of engineers and experts who have been working on this endeavor, no sound has yet been obtained that has the same sharpness and clarity as the sound perceived by the ear. Think of the highest-quality hi-fi systems produced by the largest company in the music industry. Even in these devices, when sound is recorded some of it is lost; or when you turn on a hi-fi you always hear a hissing sound before the music starts. However, the sounds that are the products of the human body's technology are extremely sharp and clear. A human ear never perceives a sound accompanied by a hissing sound or with atmospherics as does a hi-fi; rather, it perceives sound exactly as it is, sharp and clear. This is the way it has been since the creation of man.

So far, no man-made visual or recording apparatus has been as sensitive and successful in perceiving sensory data as are the eye and the ear. However, as far as seeing and hearing are concerned, a far greater truth lies beyond all this.

TO WHOM DOES THE CONSCIOUSNESS THAT SEES AND HEARS WITHIN THE BRAIN BELONG?

Who watches an alluring world in the brain, listens to symphonies and the twittering of birds, and smells the rose?

The stimulations coming from a person's eyes, ears, and nose travel to the brain as electro-chemical nerve impulses. In biology, physiology, and biochemistry books, you can find many details about how this image forms in the brain. However, you will never come across the most important fact: Who perceives these electro-chemical nerve impulses as images, sounds, odors, and sensory events in the brain?

There is a consciousness in the brain that perceives all this without feeling any need for an eye, an ear, and a nose. To whom does this consciousness belong? Of course it does not belong to the nerves, the fat layer, and neurons comprising the brain. This is why Darwinist-materialists, who believe that everything is comprised of matter, cannot answer these questions.

For this consciousness is the spirit created by Allah, which needs neither the eye to watch the images nor the ear to hear the sounds. Furthermore, it does not need the brain to think.

Everyone who reads this explicit and scientific fact should ponder on Almighty Allah, and fear and seek refuge in Him, for He squeezes the entire universe in a pitch-dark place of a few cubic centimeters in a three-dimensional, colored, shadowy, and luminous form.

A MATERIALIST FAITH

The information we have presented so far shows us that the theory of evolution is incompatible with scientific findings. The theory's claim regarding the origin of life is inconsistent with science, the evolutionary mechanisms it proposes have no evolutionary power, and fossils demonstrate that the required intermediate forms have never existed. So, it certainly follows that the theory of evolution should be pushed aside as an unscientific idea. This is how many ideas, such as the Earth-centered universe model, have been taken out of the agenda of science throughout history.

However, the theory of evolution is kept on the agenda of science. Some people even try to represent criticisms directed against it as an "attack on science." Why?

The reason is that this theory is an indispensable dogmatic belief for some circles. These circles are blindly devoted to materialist philosophy and adopt Darwinism because it is the only materialist explanation that can be put forward to explain the workings of nature.

Interestingly enough, they also confess this fact from time to time. A well-known geneticist and an outspoken evolutionist, Richard C. Lewontin from Harvard University, confesses that he is "first and foremost a materialist and then a scientist":

It is not that the methods and institutions of science somehow compel us accept a material explanation of the phenomenal world, but, on the contrary, that we are forced by our a priori adherence to material causes to create an apparatus of investigation and a set of concepts that produce material explanations, no matter how counter-intuitive, no matter how mystifying to the uninitiated. Moreover, that materialism is absolute, so we cannot allow a Divine Foot in the door.[19]

These are explicit statements that Darwinism is a dogma kept alive just for the sake of adherence to materialism. This dogma maintains that there is no being save matter. Therefore, it argues that inanimate, unconscious matter created life. It insists that millions of different living species (e.g., birds, fish, giraffes, tigers, insects, trees, flowers, whales, and human beings) originated as a result of the interactions between matter such as pouring rain, lightning flashes, and so on, out of inanimate matter. This is a precept contrary both to reason and science. Yet Darwinists continue to defend it just so as "not to allow a Divine Foot in the door."

Anyone who does not look at the origin of living beings with a materialist prejudice will see this evident truth: All living beings are works of a Creator, Who is All-Powerful, All-Wise, and All-Knowing. This Creator is Allah, Who created the whole universe from non-existence, designed it in the most perfect form, and fashioned all living beings.

THE THEORY OF EVOLUTION IS THE MOST POTENT SPELL IN THE WORLD

Anyone free of prejudice and the influence of any particular ideology, who uses only his or her reason and logic, will clearly understand that belief in the theory of evolution, which brings to mind the superstitions of societies with no knowledge of science or civilization, is quite impossible.

As explained above, those who believe in the theory of evolution think that a few atoms and molecules thrown into a huge vat could produce thinking, reasoning professors and university students; such scientists as Einstein and Galileo; such artists as Humphrey Bogart, Frank Sinatra and Luciano Pavarotti; as well as antelopes, lemon trees, and carnations. Moreover, as the scientists and professors who believe in this nonsense are educated people, it is quite justifiable to speak of this theory as "the most potent spell in history." Never before has any other belief or idea so taken away peoples' powers of reason, refused to allow them to think intelligently and logically and hidden the truth from them as if they had been blindfolded. This is an even worse and unbelievable blindness than the Egyptians worshipping the Sun God Ra, totem worship in some parts of Africa, the people of Saba worshipping the Sun, the tribe of Prophet Ibrahim (as) worshipping idols they had made with their own hands, or the people of the Prophet Musa (as) worshipping the Golden Calf.

In fact, Allah has pointed to this lack of reason in the Qur'an. He reveals in many verses that some peoples' minds will be closed and that they will be powerless to see the truth. Some of these verses are as follows:

As for those who do not believe, it makes no difference to them whether you warn them or do not warn them, they will not believe. Allah has sealed up their hearts and hearing and over their eyes is a blindfold. They will have a terrible punishment. (Surat al-Baqara, 2: 6-7)

... They have hearts with which they do not understand. They have eyes with which they do not see. They have ears with

which they do not hear. Such people are like cattle. No, they are even further astray! They are the unaware. (Surat al-A`raf, 7: 179) Even if We opened up to them a door into heaven, and they spent the day ascending through it, they would only say: "Our eyesight is befuddled! Or rather we have been put under a spell!" (Surat al-Hijr, 15: 14-15)

Words cannot express just how astonishing it is that this spell should hold such a wide community in thrall, keep people from the truth, and not be broken for 150 years. It is understandable that one or a few people might believe in impossible scenarios and claims full of stupidity and illogicality. However, "magic" is the only possible explanation for people from all over the world believing that unconscious and lifeless atoms suddenly decided to come together and form a universe that functions with a flawless system of organization, discipline, reason, and consciousness; a planet named Earth with all of its features so perfectly suited to life; and living things full of countless complex systems.

In fact, the Qur'an relates the incident of Prophet Musa (as) and Pharaoh to show that some people who support atheistic philosophies actually influence others by magic. When Pharaoh was told about the true religion, he told Prophet Musa (as) to meet with his own magicians. When Musa (as) did so, he told them to demonstrate their abilities first. The verses continue:

He said: "You throw." And when they threw, they cast a spell on the people's eyes and caused them to feel great fear of them. They produced an extremely powerful magic. (Surat al-A`raf, 7: 116)

As we have seen, Pharaoh's magicians were able to deceive everyone, apart from Musa (as) and those who believed in him. However, his evidence broke the spell, or "swallowed up what they had forged," as the verse puts it.

We revealed to Musa, "Throw down your staff." And it immediately swallowed up what they had forged. So the Truth took place and what they did was shown to be false. (Surat al-A`raf, 7: 117-118)

As we can see, when people realized that a spell had been cast upon them and that what they saw was just an illusion, Pharaoh's magicians lost all credibility. In the present day too, unless those who, under the influence of a similar spell, believe in these ridiculous claims under their scientific disguise and spend their lives defending them, abandon their superstitious beliefs, they also will be humiliated when the full truth emerges and the spell is broken. In fact, world-renowned British writer and philosopher Malcolm Muggeridge also stated this:

I myself am convinced that the theory of evolution, especially the extent to which it's been applied, will be one of the great jokes in the history books in the future. Posterity will marvel that so very flimsy and dubious an hypothesis could be accepted with the incredible credulity that it has.[20]

That future is not far off: On the contrary, people will soon see that "chance" is not a deity, and will look back on the theory of evolution as the worst deceit and the most terrible spell in the world. That spell is already rapidly beginning to be lifted from the shoulders of people all over the world. Many people who see its true face are wondering with amazement how they could ever have been taken in by it.

They said 'Glory be to You!
We have no knowledge except what
You have taught us.
You are the All-Knowing,
the All-Wise.'
(Surat al-Baqara: 32)

NOTES

1 Sidney Fox, Klaus Dose, *Molecular Evolution and The Origin of Life*, W.H. Freeman and Company, San Francisco, 1972, p. 4.
2 Alexander I. Oparin, *Origin of Life*, Dover Publications, NewYork, 1936, 1953 (reprint), p. 196.
3 "New Evidence on Evolution of Early Atmosphere and Life", *Bulletin of the American Meteorological Society*, vol 63, November 1982, p. 1328-1330.
4 Stanley Miller, *Molecular Evolution of Life: Current Status of the Prebiotic Synthesis of Small Molecules*, 1986, p. 7.
5 Jeffrey Bada, *Earth*, February 1998, p. 40.
6 Leslie E. Orgel, "The Origin of Life on Earth", *Scientific American*, vol. 271, October 1994, p. 78.
7 Charles Darwin, *The Origin of Species by Means of Natural Selection*, The Modern Library, New York, p. 127.
8 Charles Darwin, *The Origin of Species: A Facsimile of the First Edition*, Harvard University Press, 1964, p. 184.
9 B. G. Ranganathan, *Origins?*, Pennsylvania: The Banner Of Truth Trust, 1988, p. 7.
10 Charles Darwin, *The Origin of Species: A Facsimile of the First Edition*, Harvard University Press, 1964, p. 179.
11 Derek A. Ager, "The Nature of the Fossil Record", *Proceedings of the British Geological Association*, vol 87, 1976, p. 133.
12 Douglas J. Futuyma, *Science on Trial*, Pantheon Books, New York, 1983. p. 197.
13 Solly Zuckerman, *Beyond The Ivory Tower*, Toplinger Publications, New York, 1970, pp. 75-14; Charles E. Oxnard, "The Place of Australopithecines in Human Evolution: Grounds for Doubt", Nature, vol 258, p. 389.
14 "Could science be brought to an end by scientists' belief that they have final answers or by society's reluctance to pay the bills?" *Scientific American*, December 1992, p. 20.
15 Alan Walker, *Science*, vol. 207, 7 March 1980, p. 1103; A. J. Kelso, *Physical Antropology*, 1st ed., J. B. Lipincott Co., New York, 1970, p. 221; M. D. Leakey, Olduvai Gorge, vol. 3, Cambridge University Press, Cambridge, 1971, p. 272.
16 Jeffrey Kluger, "Not So Extinct After All: The Primitive Homo Erectus May Have Survived Long Enough To Coexist With Modern Humans", *Time*, 23 December 1996.
17 S. J. Gould, *Natural History*, vol. 85, 1976, p. 30.
18 Solly Zuckerman, *Beyond The Ivory Tower*, p. 19.
19 Richard Lewontin, "The Demon-Haunted World," "The New York: Toplinger Publications, 1970, 19.
20 Malcolm Muggeridge, *The End of Christendom*, Grand Rapids: Eerdmans, 1980, p. 43.

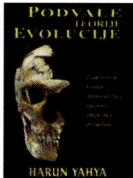

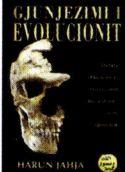

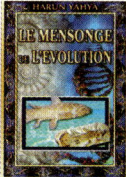

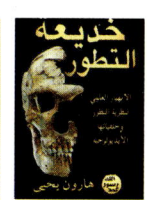

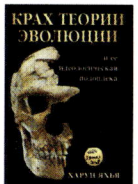

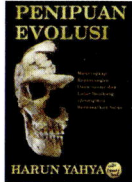

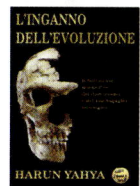

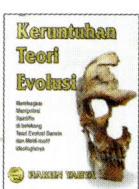

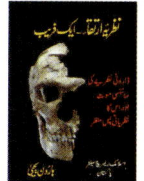

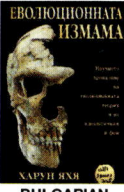

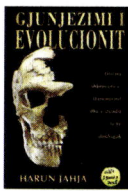

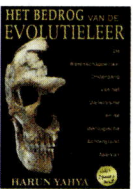

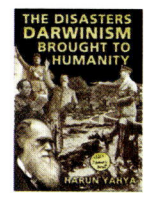

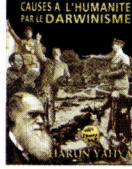

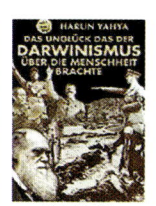

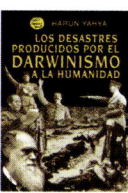

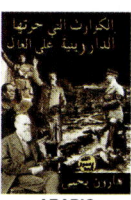

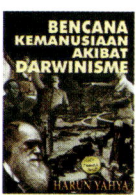

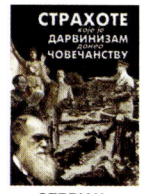

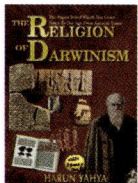

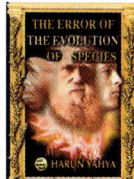

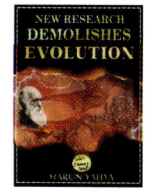

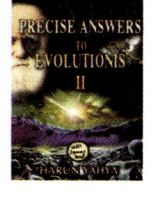

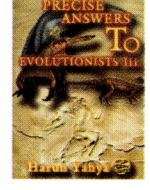

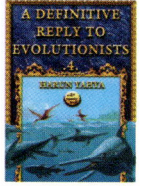

ALSO BY HARUN YAHYA

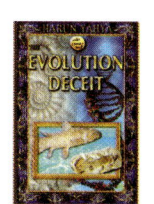

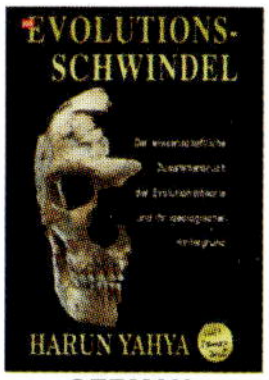

FRENCH INDONESIAN

GERMAN INDONESIAN MALAY

BOSNIAN

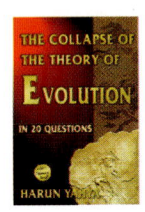

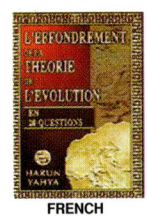

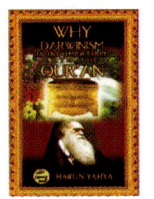

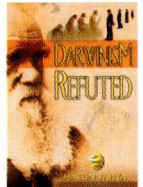

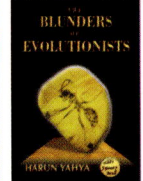

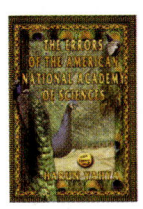

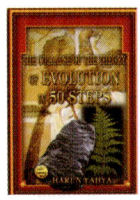

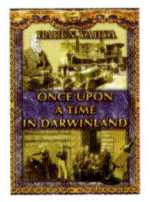

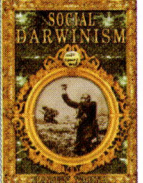

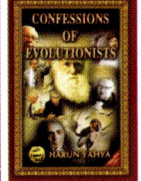

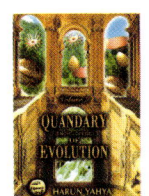

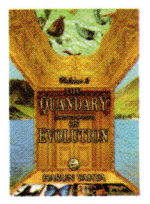

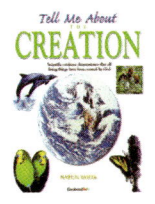

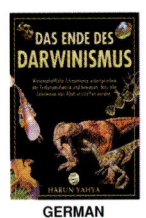

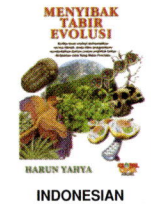

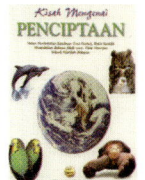

INDONESIAN BOSNIAN

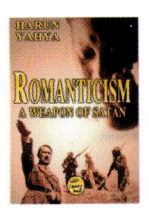

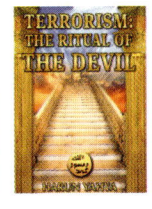

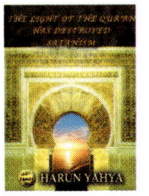

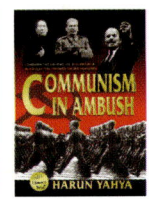

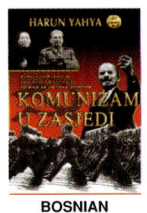

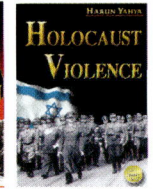

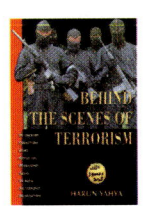

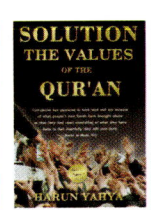

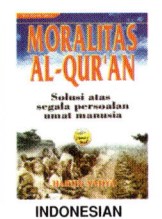

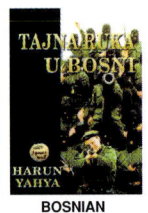

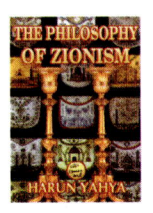

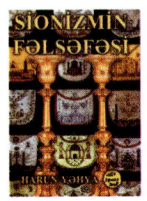

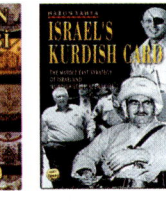

AZERI

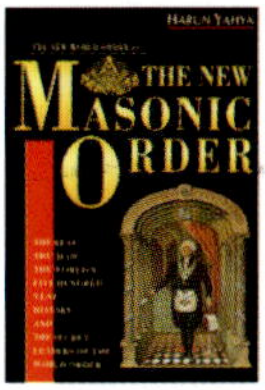

AZERI

GERMAN

BOSNIAN

RUSSIAN

AZERI

INDONESIAN

CHINESE

ALBANIAN

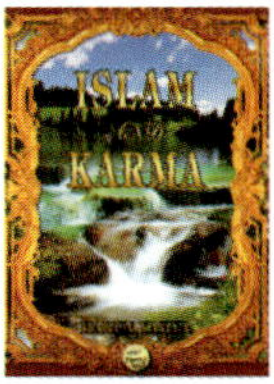

AZERI

AZERI

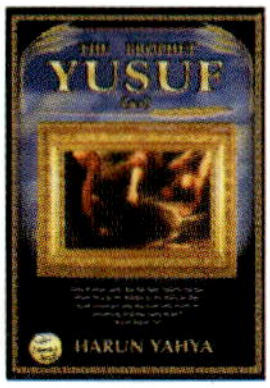

GERMAN

AZERI

AZERI

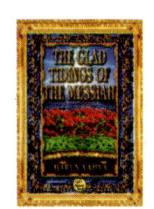

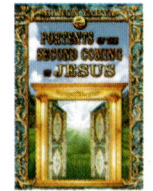

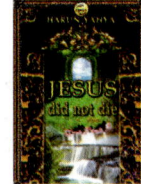

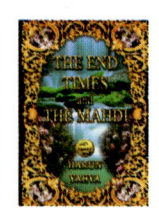

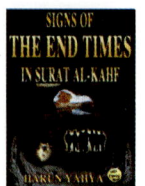

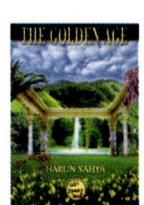

AZERI 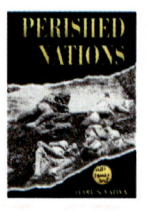 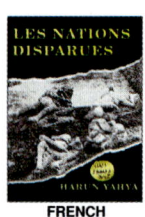 — FRENCH 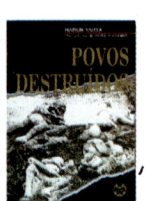 — PORTUGUESE

GERMAN  — SPANISH 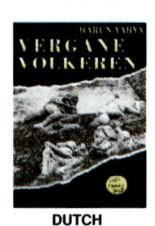 — DUTCH 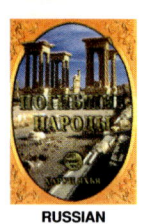 — RUSSIAN  — INDONESIAN  — ARABIC

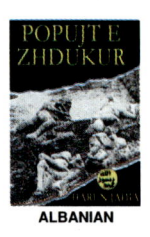

ALBANIAN 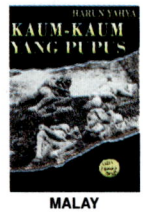 — MALAY 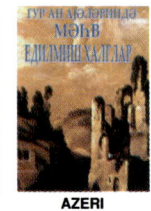 — AZERI 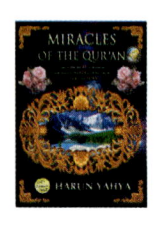 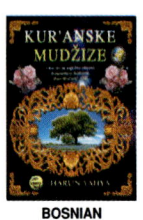 — BOSNIAN 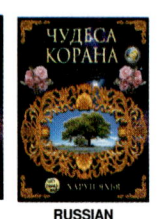 — RUSSIAN

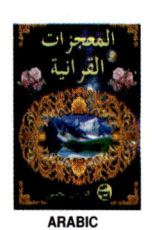

ARABIC  — ALBANIAN  — CHINESE 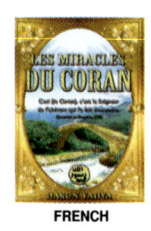 — FRENCH  — INDONESIAN 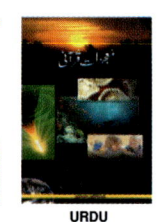 — URDU

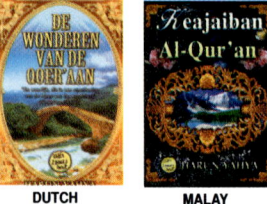

DUTCH — MALAY  — AZERI 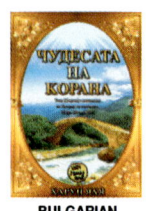 — BULGARIAN 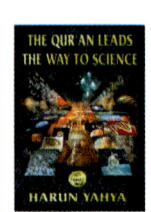 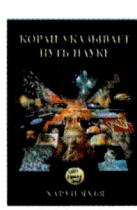 — RUSSIAN

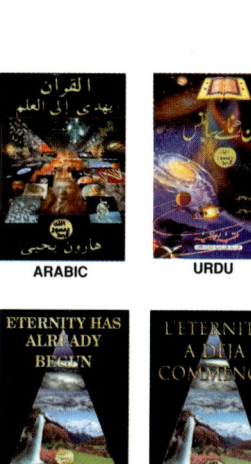

| ARABIC | URDU | 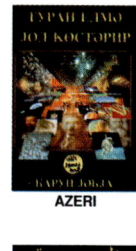 AZERI | | DUTCH | ARABIC |

| | FRENCH | ARABIC | URDU | INDONESIAN | |

| URDU | | | | GERMAN | |

| URDU | FRENCH | 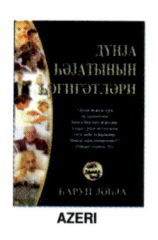 AZERI | | FRENCH | PERSIAN |

| ARABIC | 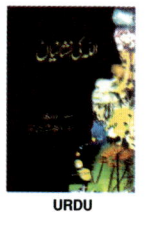 URDU | INDONESIAN | AZERI | | FRENCH |

| INDONESIAN | ARABIC | ALBANIAN | |  RUSSIAN |  ARABIC |

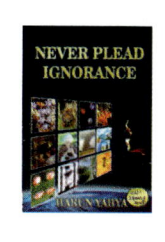

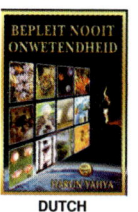

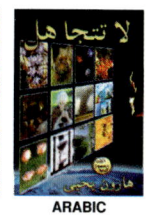

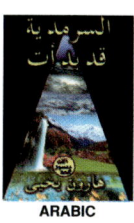

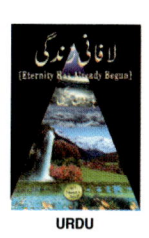

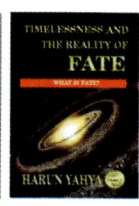

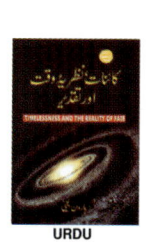

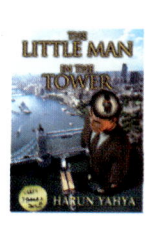

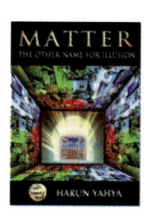

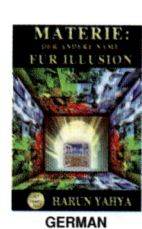

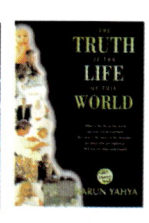

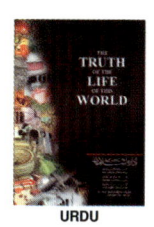

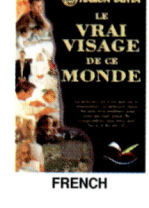

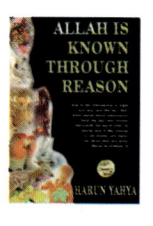

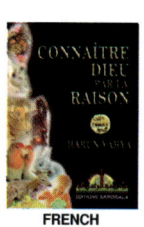

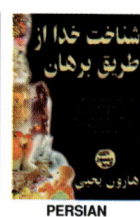

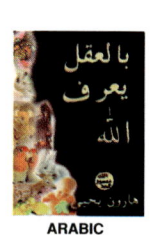

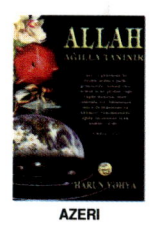

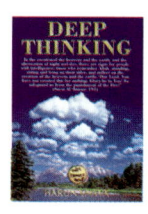

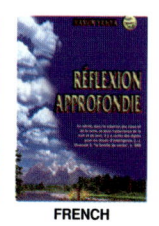

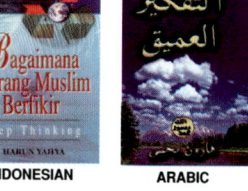

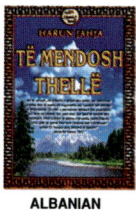

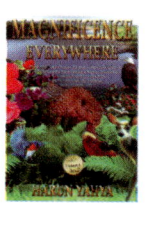

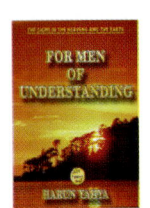

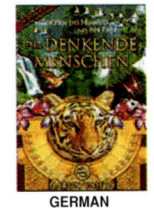

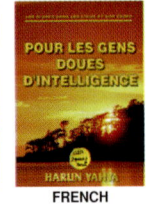

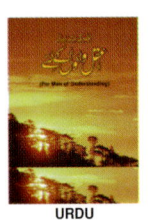

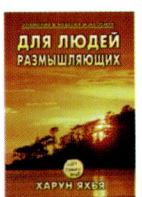

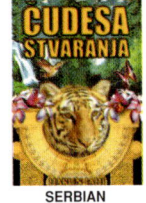

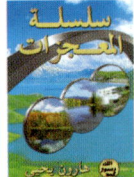

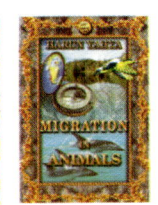

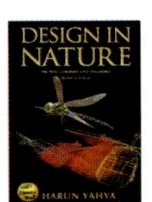

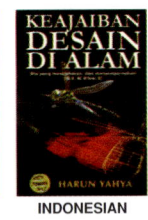

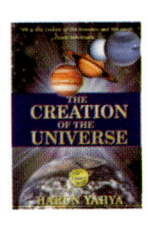

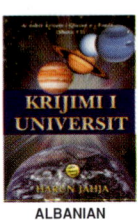

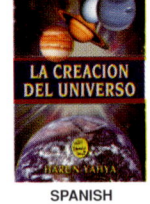

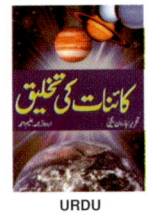

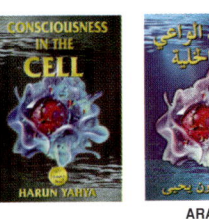

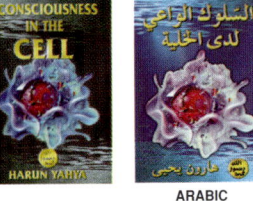

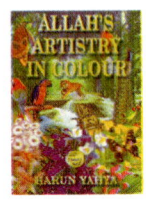

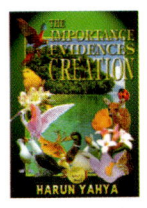

FOR MEN OF UNDERSTANDING	GERMAN	FRENCH	URDU	RUSSIAN	INDONESIAN	
SPANISH	SERBIAN	DANISH	ALBANIAN		ARABIC	
		RUSSIAN	INDONESIAN	ARABIC		
	FRENCH	RUSSIAN	GERMAN	ALBANIAN	CHINESE	
INDONESIAN	SPANISH	ARABIC	URDU		ARABIC	
				ARABIC	INDONESIAN	

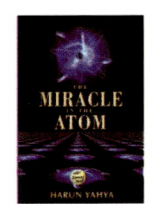

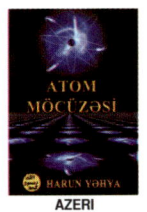

THE MIRACLE IN THE ATOM	ČUDO ATOMA	 Keajaiban pada Atom	ATOM MÖCÜZƏSI	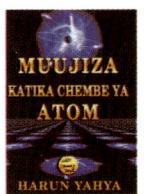 MUUJIZA KATIKA CHEMBE YA ATOM	ALLAH'S ART OF AFFECTION	
	SERBIAN	INDONESIAN	AZERI	KISWAHILI		

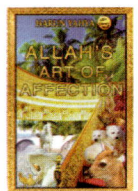

THE MIRACLE OF TALKING BIRDS	THE MIRACLE OF BLOOD AND THE HEART	DEVOTION AMONG ANIMALS	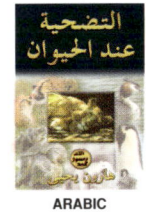 التضحية عند الحيوان	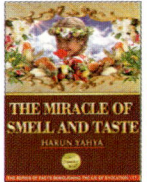 THE MIRACLE OF SMELL AND TASTE	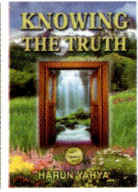 KNOWING THE TRUTH
			ARABIC		

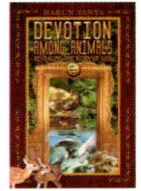

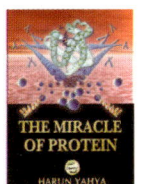 THE MIRACLE OF PROTEIN	 THE GREEN MIRACLE PHOTOSYNTHESIS	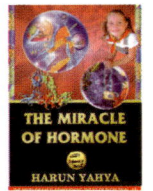 THE MIRACLE OF HORMONE	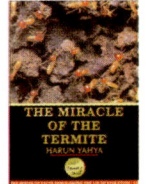 THE MIRACLE OF THE TERMITE	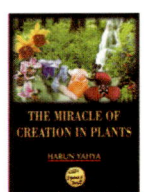 THE MIRACLE OF CREATION IN PLANTS	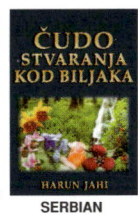 ČUDO STVARANJA KOD BILJAKA
					SERBIAN

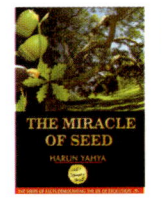 THE MIRACLE OF SEED	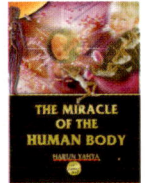 THE MIRACLE OF THE HUMAN BODY	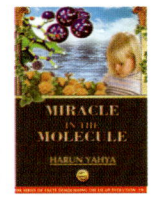 MIRACLE IN THE MOLECULE	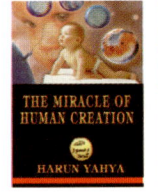 THE MIRACLE OF HUMAN CREATION	 معجزة خلق الإنسان	 KEAJAIBAN PENCIPTAAN MANUSIA
				ARABIC	INDONESIAN

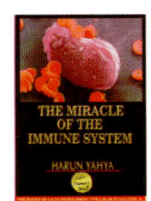 THE MIRACLE OF THE IMMUNE SYSTEM	 Sistem Kekebalan Tubuh	LE MIRACLE DU SYSTEME IMMUNITAIRE	 ČUDO IMUNOG SISTEMA	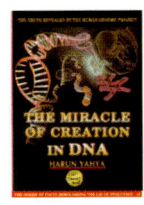 THE MIRACLE OF CREATION IN DNA	LE MIRACLE DE LA CREATION DANS L'ADN
	INDONESIAN	FRENCH	SERBIAN		FRENCH

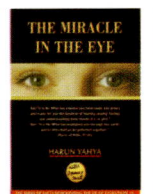

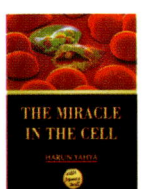

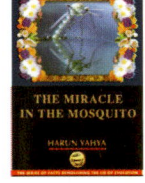

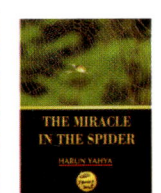

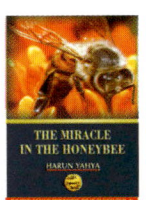

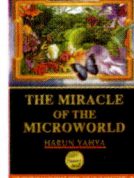

THE MIRACLE IN THE EYE	THE MIRACLE IN THE CELL	THE MIRACLE IN THE MOSQUITO	THE MIRACLE IN THE SPIDER	THE MIRACLE IN THE HONEYBEE	THE MIRACLE OF THE MICROWORLD	

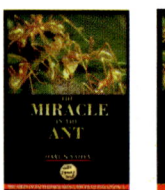

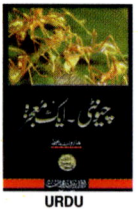

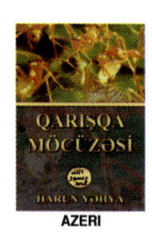

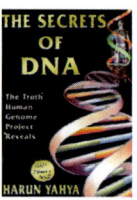

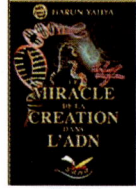

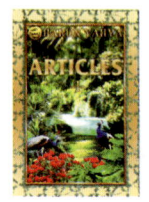

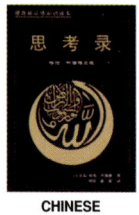

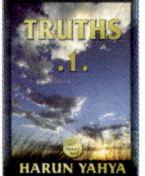

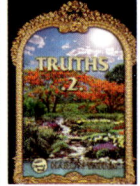

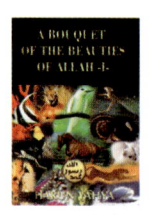

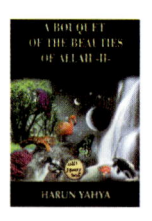

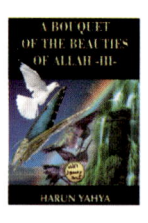

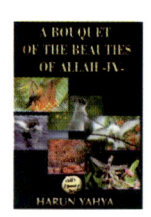

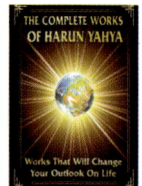

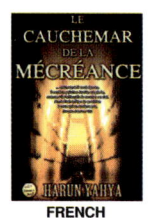

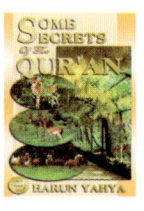

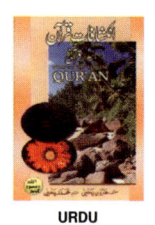

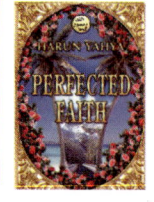

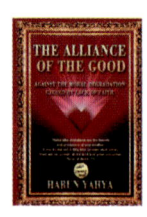

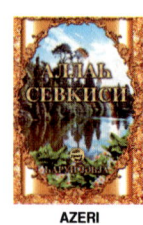

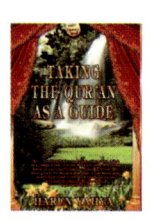

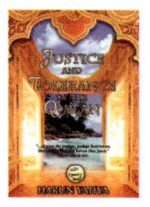

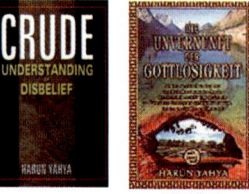

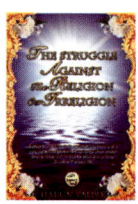

	URDU	INDONESIAN	AZERI			FRENCH
			INDONESIAN	CHINESE		
		FRENCH		URDU	FRENCH	
					GERMAN	AZERI
		GERMAN	INDONESIAN		INDONESIAN	

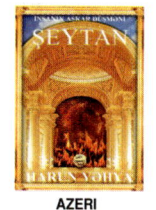

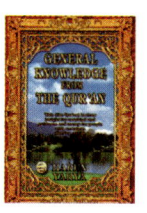

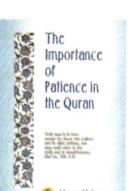

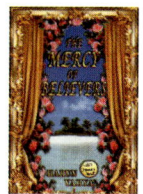

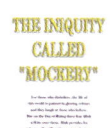

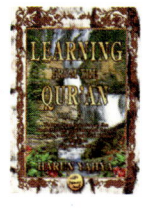

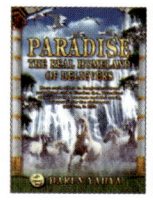

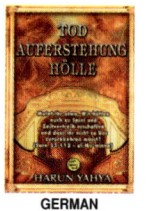

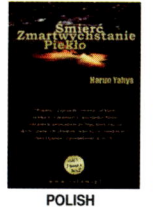

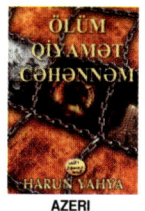

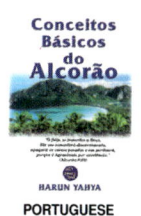

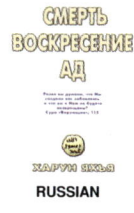

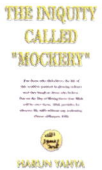

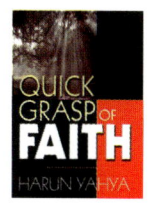

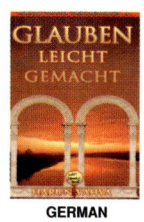

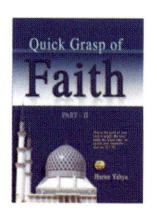

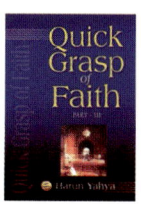

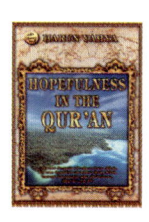

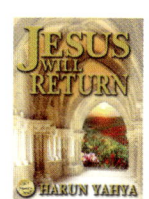

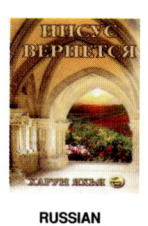

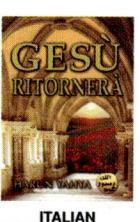

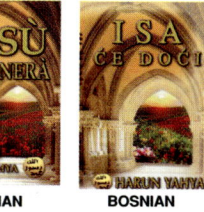

SATAN	SEYTAN — AZERI	NEVER FORGET
GENERAL KNOWLEDGE FROM THE QUR'AN	The Importance of Patience in the Quran	THE MERCY OF BELIEVERS
THE ENTHUSIASM DISPLAYED IN THE QUR'AN	THE INIQUITY CALLED "MOCKERY"	NAMES OF ALLAH
LEARNING FROM THE QUR'AN	PARADISE THE BELIEVERS' REAL HOME	MOONLIGHTS OF VERSES — AZERI
Death Resurrection Hell	TOD AUFERSTEHUNG HÖLLE — GERMAN	Śmierć Zmartwychwstanie Piekło — POLISH
ÖLÜM QIYAMƏT CƏHƏNNƏM — AZERI	Conceitos Básicos do Alcorão — PORTUGUESE	СМЕРТЬ ВОСКРЕСЕНИЕ АД — RUSSIAN
OUR MESSENGERS SAY	THE INIQUITY CALLED "MOCKERY"	COMMONLY DISREGARDED QUR'ANIC RULINGS
SINCERITY DESCRIBED IN THE QUR'AN	KEIKHLASAN dalam Telaah Al-Qur'an — INDONESIAN	THE THEORY OF EVOLUTION
QUICK GRASP OF FAITH	GLAUBEN LEICHT GEMACHT — GERMAN	Quick Grasp of faith CARA CEPAT MEMAHAMI IMAN 1 — INDONESIAN
Quick Grasp of Faith PART II	Quick Grasp of Faith PART III	HOPEFULNESS IN THE QUR'AN
JESUS WILL RETURN	JESUS WIRD KOMMEN — GERMAN	ИИСУС ВЕРНЕТСЯ — RUSSIAN
GESÙ RITORNERÀ — ITALIAN	ISA ĆE DOĆI — BOSNIAN	YESUS AKAN KEMBALI — INDONESIAN

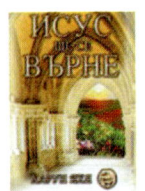

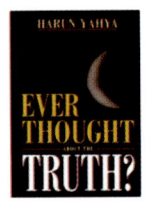

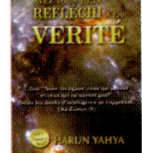

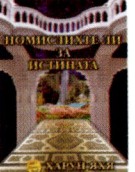

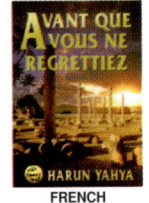

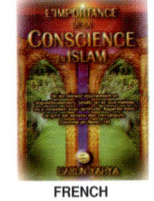

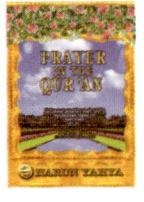

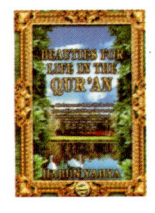

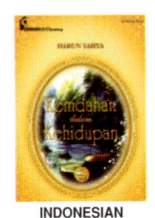

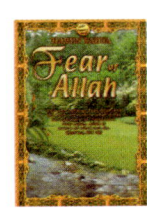

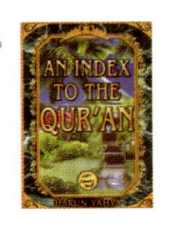

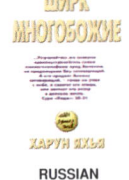

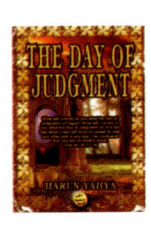

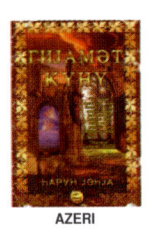

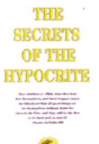

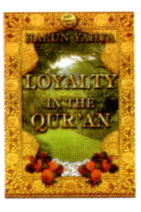

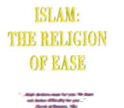

BULGARIAN	PORTUGUESE		FRENCH	BULGARIAN	URDU
	GERMAN	FRENCH	AZERI	INDONESIAN	
	GERMAN	FRENCH	ARABIC	INDONESIAN	
	INDONESIAN			RUSSIAN	
		RUSSIAN		AZERI	
			RUSSIAN		

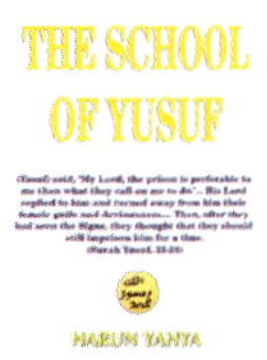

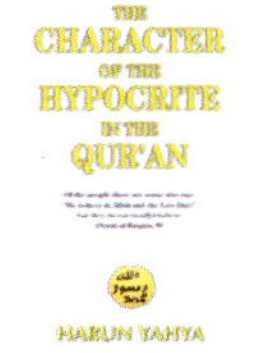

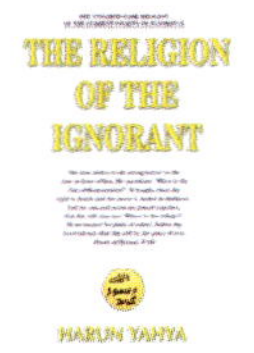

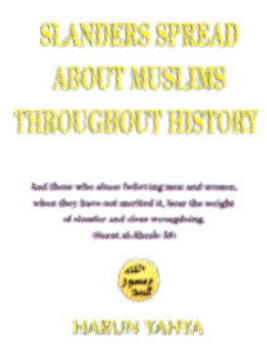

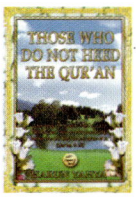

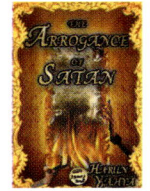

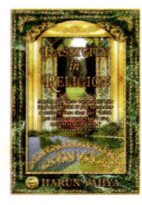

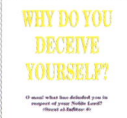

THE SCHOOL OF YUSUF	THE CHARACTER OF THE HYPOCRITE IN THE QUR'AN	THE RELIGION OF THE IGNORANT	A LURKING THREAT HEEDLESSNESS	ABANDONING THE SOCIETY OF IGNORANCE	SLANDERS SPREAD ABOUT MUSLIMS THROUGHOUT HISTORY	

HUMAN CHARACTERS IN THE SOCIETY OF IGNORANCE	THOSE WHO DO NOT HEED THE QUR'AN	THE ARROGANCE OF SATAN	PERISHED NATIONS	WHY DO YOU DECEIVE YOURSELF?	ЗАЧЕМ ТЫ ВВОДИШЬ СЕБЯ В ЗАБЛУЖДЕНИЕ? RUSSIAN	

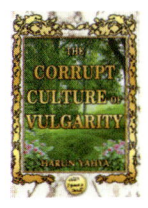

THE CORRUPT CULTURE OF VULGARITY	THE MORAL VALUES OF THE QURAN	কুরআনে নৈতিক মূল্যবোধ BENGOLI	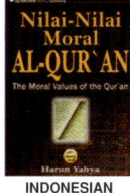 Nilai-Nilai Moral AL-QUR'AN INDONESIAN	COMMUNICATING THE MESSAGE AND DISPUTING IN THE QUR'AN	QURANDA TƏBLIĞ VƏ MÜBAHİSƏ AZERI	

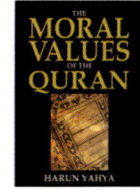

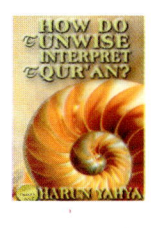 HOW DO UNWISE INTERPRET THE QUR'AN?	COMMENT LES INCRÉDULES INTERPRÈTENT-ILS LE CORAN? FRENCH	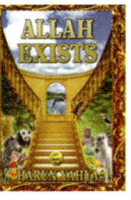 ALLAH EXISTS	THE SILENT LANGUAGE OF EVIL	AGONIES OF A FAKE WORLD	ANSWERS FROM THE QUR'AN	

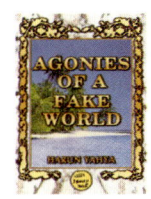

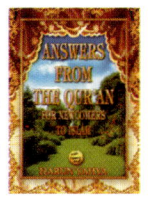

The Basic Concepts in the Quran	LES CONCEPTS FONDAMENTAUX DANS LE SAINT CORAN FRENCH	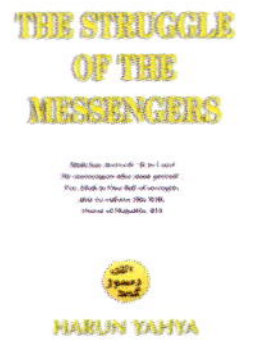 THE STRUGGLE OF THE MESSENGERS	THOSE WHO EXHAUST THEIR PLEASURES DURING THEIR WORLDLY LIVES	THE HAPPINESS OF BELIEVERS	THE SOLUTION TO SECRET TORMENTS	

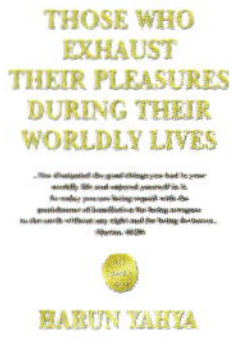

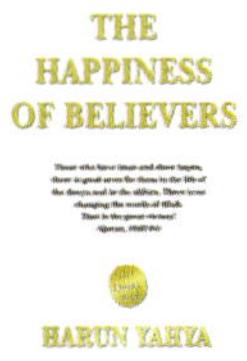

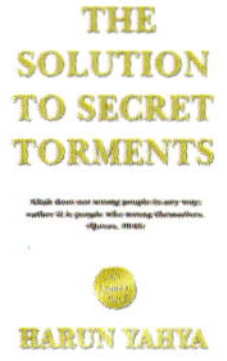

CHILDREN'S BOOKS

THE IMPORTANCE OF FOLLOWING THE Good Word	TRUE WISDOM DESCRIBED IN THE QUR'AN	DEAR KIDS HAVE YOU EVER THOUGHT? 4 LET'S LEARN OUR ISLAM	DEAR KIDS, HAVE YOU EVER THOUGHT? 2 the glory in the heavens	РЕБЯТА, А ЗНАЕТЕ ЛИ ВЫ ОБ ЭТОМ? ВЕЛИКОЛЕПИЕ В НЕБЕСАХ RUSSIAN	رحلة في الكون ARABIC	

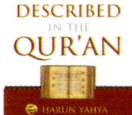

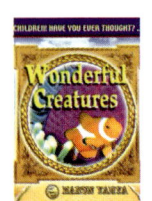

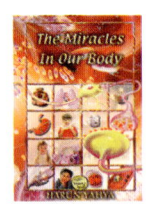

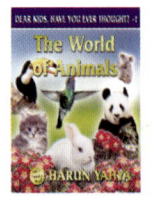

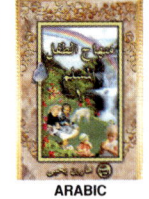

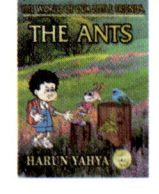

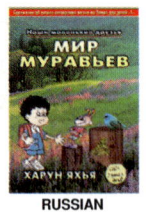

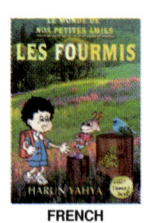

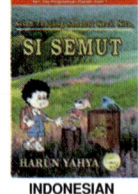

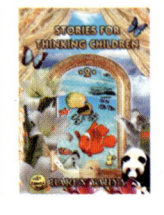

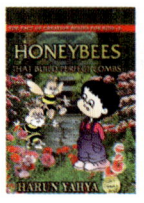

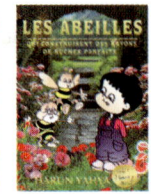

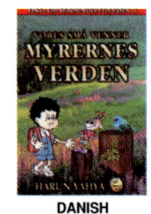

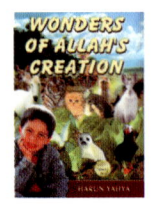

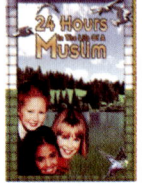

	ARABIC	AZERI		INDONESIAN	GERMAN	
	ARABIC		FRENCH	RUSSIAN	ARABIC	
	ARABIC		RUSSIAN	FRENCH	INDONESIAN	
ARABIC	DANISH		ARABIC		GERMAN	
RUSSIAN	BOSNIAN	INDONESIAN	FRENCH		ARABIC	DANISH
	INDONESIAN	SERBIAN		ARABIC		ARABIC

HARUN YAHYA POCKET BOOK SERIES

AUDIO CASETTE SERIES

THE FACT OF CREATION

The titles in this series include The Theory of Evolution The Fact of Creation, The Creation of the Universe/The Balances in the Earth, The Miracle in the Cell/The Miracle of Birth, The Miracle in the Eye/The Miracle in the Ear, The Design in Animals/The Design in Plants, The Miracle in the Honeybee/The Miracle in the Ant, The Miracle in the Mosquito/ The Miracle in the Spider, Self-Sacrifice in Living Things /Migration and Orientation, The Miracle of Creation in DNA, Miracles of the Qur'an.

EVER THOUGHT ABOUT THE TRUTH? I

The titles in this series include Ever Thought About the Truth?, Devoted to Allah, The Mature Faith, The Religion of the Ignorant, The Crude Understanding of Disbelief, The Importance of Conscience in the Qur'an, Never Forget, Before You Regret, Death Hereafter Hell, Paradise.

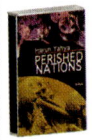

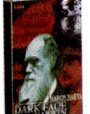

The audio cassettes Perished Nations and The Dark Face of Darwin were inspired by the works of Harun Yahya

EVER THOUGHT ABOUT THE TRUTH? II

The titles in this series include The Fear of Allah, The Nightmare of Disbelief, The Struggle of the Religion of Irreligion, Beauties Presented by the Qur'an for Life, The Arrogance of Satan, The Mercy of Believers, The Iniquity Called Mockery, Perished Nations, The Secret Beyond Matter, Timelessness and The Reality of Fate.

The Collapse of Evolution The Fact of Creation audio cassette is also available in Russian.

AUDIO CD SERIES

The Miracle in the Ant - The Miracle in the Honeybee

The Basic Concepts in the Qur'an

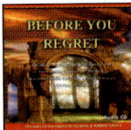

Before You Regret

The Miracle in the Cell The Miracle in the Birth

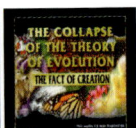

The Collapse of the Theory of Evolution

The Importance of Conscience in the Qur'an

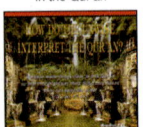

How Do the Unwise Interpret the Qur'an?

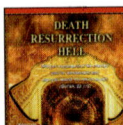

Death, Resurrection, Hell

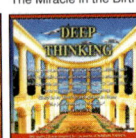

Deep Thinking

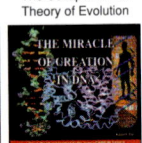

The Miracle of Creation in DNA

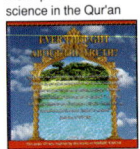

Ever Thought About the Truth?

The Miracle in the Ear The Miracle in the Eye

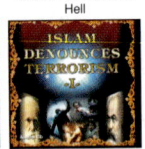

Islam Denounces Terrorism 1

Islam Denounces Terrorism 2

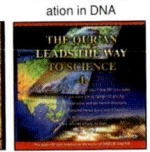

The Qur'an Leads the Way to Science 1

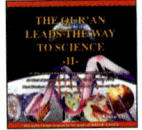

The Qur'an Leads the Way to Science 2

Miracles of the Qur'an

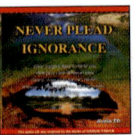

Never Plead Ignorance

The Nightmare of Disbelief

Romanticism: A Weapon of Satan 1

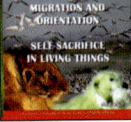

Romanticism: A Weapon of Satan 2

Migration and Orientation Self-Sacrifice in Living Things

Some Secrets of the Quran

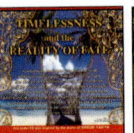

Timelessness and the Reality of Fate

The Miracle in the Spider The Miracle in the Mosquito

DOCUMENTARY FILMS

All documentary films are available as DVD, VCD, VHS format. Order from:
www.bookglobal.net   e-mail: info@bookglobal.net

Fact of Creation Series

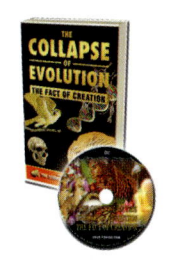

- The Collapse of Evolution Fact of Creation
- The Secret Beyond Matter 
- The Creation of the Universe 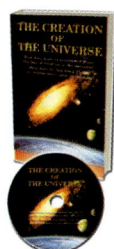
- The Miracle Planet 1 
- The Miracle Planet 2 
- Splendour in the Seas 
- The Miracle in Birds 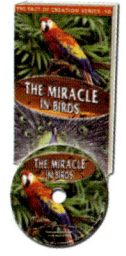
- For Men of Understanding 1
- For Men of Understanding 2
- For Men of Understanding 3 
- The Miracle in the Cell 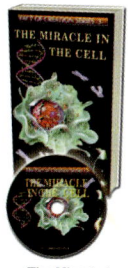
- The Fact of Creation 
- The Miracle in the Ant 
- The Miracle of Man's Creation 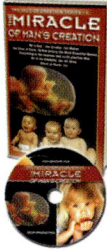
- Architects in Nature 
- The Order of the Heavens 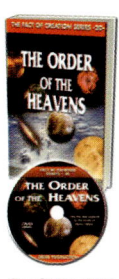
- Altruism in Nature 
- Love and Cooperation in Living Things 

- Allah is Known Through Reason
- The Miracle of Seed
- Miracles of Brain: Smell and Taste
- Biomimetics: Technology Imitates Nature
- The Miracle of Respiration
- World of Ice
- Technology in Nature
- Miracles of the Qur'an
- The Secret of the Test
- The Truth of the Life of this World
- Perished Nations 1 - 2
- Answers From the Qur'an 1 - 2 - 3
- Deep Thinking,
- Solution: The Values of the Qur'an
- The Names of Allah
- The End Times and the Mahdi
- Signs of the Last Day
- The Qur'an Leads the Way to Science
- The Disasters Darwinism Brought to Humanity
- Satanism Satan's Bloody Teaching
- The Bloody History of Communism 1 - 2 - 3
- The Collapse of Atheism,
- Behind the Veil of War,
- Islam Denounces Terrorism,
- The Philosophy of Zionism

HARUN YAHYA ON THE INTERNET

www.harunyahya.com
e-mail: info@harunyahya.com

YOU CAN PURCHASE HARUN YAHYA'S BOOKS FROM THIS SITE!

www.bookglobal.net
e-mail: info@bookglobal.net

www.islamdenouncesterrorism.com

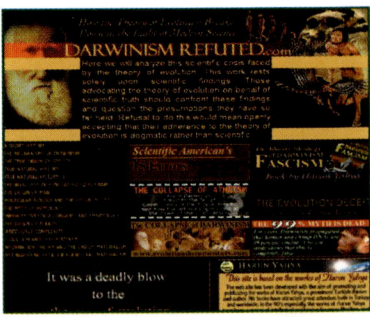

www.darwinismrefuted.com

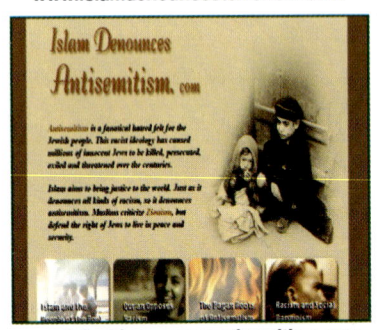

www.islamdenouncesantisemitism.com

www.jesuswillreturn.com

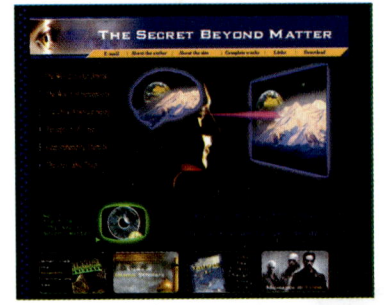

www.secretbeyondmatter.com

www.unionoffaiths.com
www.perishednations.com
www.miraclesofthequran.com
www.darwinism-watch.com
www.insight-magazine.com
www.theprophetmuhammad.org
www.palestiniantragedy.com
www.truthsforkids.com
www.for-children.com
www.evolutiondeceit.com